FREE-FORM BARGELLO

FREE-FORM BARGELLO

by Gigs Stevens

Charles Scribner's Sons, New York

Library of Congress Cataloging in Publication Data
Stevens, Gigs.
    Free-form bargello.

    1. Canvas embroidery. I. Title.
TT778.C3S73   746.4'4   77-5784
ISBN 0-684-15024-7
ISBN 0-684-15055-7 pbk.

1 3 5 7 9 11 13 15 17 19 MD/P 20 18 16 14 12 10 8 6 4 2
1 3 5 7 9 11 13 15 17 19 MD/C 20 18 16 14 12 10 8 6 4 2

Printed in the United States of America

Selected stanzas on page 28 from "What Is Pink?," "What Is
Brown?," "What Is Gray?," "What Is Green?," "What Is Gold?,"
"What Is White?," and "What Is Purple?" in HAILSTONES
AND HALIBUT BONES by Mary O'Neill. Copyright © 1961
Mary Le Duc O'Neill. Reprinted by permission of Doubleday
& Company, Inc.

To Steve, who listened for endless hours, nimbly alleviating my concerns and building my confidence.

To Piper, whose sensitive interest, coupled with his own creative approaches, always relieved stagnancy.

To Larkin, whose quiet confidence in my book's success made its completion inevitable and obvious.

To Courtney, whose inventive, appealing drawings provided the springboards for new interpretations.

To Hunter, who was the first to list my occupation as "author," in addition to "mother" and "homemaker."

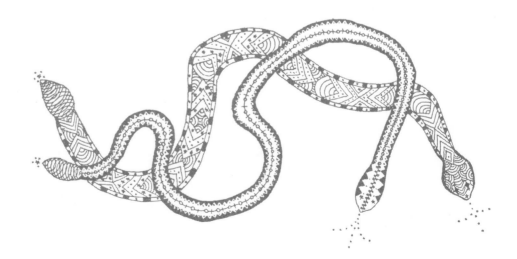

ACKNOWLEDGMENTS

So many stitchers have plied threads with inexorable patience and boundless enthusiasm, always buoying my spirits and helping me make my book a reality rather than a dreamy topic of conversation. What a myriad of tangents have emerged on this ever-widening circle of needlework.

The real importance of encouragement was unknown to me before this project. The support of family and friends was most gratifying. The unexpected sustenance from far-flung needles added impetus when I struggled against indecision, apprehension, and self-doubt.

My thanks to Elinor Parker, whose inexhaustible patience and serenity, coupled with velvet guidance, always made my monumental problems seem trifles hardly worth considering.

To Michael Myers, whose impeccable judgment, combined with technical skill, produced photographs of superior quality and accurate color reproduction.

To Eye Squared and Katherine Stone, that beautiful woman who made the result of our amalgamation amelioristic.

My grateful thanks also to the enthusiastic and willing stitchers who worked this untested method of needlepoint and helped iron out the kinks with relentless endurance: Lee Bogart, Jeanne Childs, Catherine Gemmell, Cecile Gudelsky, Janet Larkin, Leona Myers, Addie Robb, Phyllis Schain, Kate Stone, and Lissa Sullivan.

The two artists who executed the line drawings were a constant source of inspiration: Melissa L. Van Schoonhoven and Courtney C. Stevens.

The painting of the zebra head (Plate 18) was used with the kind permission of the artist, Countess Cis Zoltowska.

The shark's jaws (Plate 29) were drawn by my favorite shark fisherman and expert, Raymond D. Stevens, Jr.

Photo on page 32 and Plate 31 were photographed by Ernest Beadle, courtesy *House and Garden*, Copyright © 1976 by Condé Nast Publications, Inc.

Contents

"It's an old-fashioned cure for restlessness, my dear, in case you ever need it. I haven't travelled without my tapestry since girlhood, and you should see the testimonials to worries of all sorts. Whenever I have felt nervous, vaguely dissatisfied, irresolute or frankly wretched, I have sat by myself. Each embroidery contains hundreds of stitches which are the cross-stones of sorrow, the death beds of boredom.

In many a gaily flowered seat, my unhappiness lies buried. People spend time and money on being exorcised; psycho-analysed, they call it, seeking relief for body and soul. I think that a good long mechanical task that requires a minimum of attention, and the soothing action of the hand as it dips over and under the canvas, is the very best means of pinning down our weaknesses and chloroforming them. Stitch the horrors down, my dear, and they shan't return to plague you; they are killed by a stab of the needle. During peaceful intervals, I have laid my work away for months, but when I need it, there it is, convenient as a box of aspirins against a cold."

Introduction

For any disciple of needlepoint, there comes a time to venture forth using traditional methods as the vehicle to explore and enjoy new frontiers of design and composition. Such a call beckoned me, and in the chapters that follow you will share with me the excitement of free-form bargello.

Rather than being bound by the more structured patterns we've all executed with great satisfaction (but perhaps a little boredom), creative bargello is a fresh approach but does not totally abandon all the old rules. The joy I've found in it springs from its freedom and tremendous element of surprise as each phase of the design develops. To gain familiarity, you can take patterns from graphs; but as your confidence grows, a more adventuresome spirit is sure to prevail with astonishing results.

My early experimentation with free-form bargello quickly dispelled the notion that the result should, or even could, be perceived at the outset. After discarding many preplanned canvases, I found that the greatest success derives from exercising a daring and bold freedom in the selection of color and form. Using my technique, you tend to mold the canvas, rather than stitch it.

As the following pages suggest, the careful selection of color is just about the only prerequisite, but changes even in the color scheme can be made as the work progresses and the pattern unfolds. By its very nature the bargello stitch enables you to move along swiftly in the knowledge that as formations take shape, you experience the intrigue of a good mystery story. To me, it's the element of discovery that is especially appealing, and it's a change of pace from the painted canvas, which, while a gratifying accomplishment, is necessarily disciplined in its execution. Flexibility and uniqueness of results, therefore, are important characteristics that set free-form bargello apart from other needlepoint techniques.

This book emphasizes the limitless possibilities to be achieved through color and shape. Bright, contrasting colors, soft pastel combinations, and even monochromatic blends are discussed in terms of their influence on form and the expansion of a theme. In addition, textural variations provided by the use of linen, metallics, silk, and other media will be introduced as ever so subtle accents to add a tasteful third dimension to your work. Even the neophyte need not have qualms over experimentation opportunities presented herein. The use of photocopying techniques and other hints are provided to bring free-form bargello well within the grasp of those possessing even the most elementary skills.

From your first endeavor on, I know you'll sense the joy of innovation as the bargello moves, envelops, and explodes a central theme with a grace and strength far beyond the capacity of any other background stitch.

History of bargello

The history of bargello is shrouded in mystery and fable. Even the name itself sounds strange and awkward. It is fairly well established that bargello was being executed to great advantage in sixteenth-century Florence, most often on even-weave linen, as opposed to the mono canvas mesh we use. Particularly beautiful chairs thought to have been stitched around that period are still on view in the Bargello Palace in Florence. Wild, imaginative tales pronounce that they were done by prisoners in death row in jail—a rather incredible idea if you consider the patience and serenity necessary for smooth stitching.

Bargello is also referred to as Hungarian Point. Legend holds that a Hungarian princess, the bride of a Florentine nobleman, brought the method with her from Hungary. Many pieces of her trousseau were trimmed in Hungarian Point. The ladies of the court were enchanted with it and set about to copy and expand on the new method of handwork.

The origin of references to bargello as flame stitch is obvious, especially on the wonderful wing chairs and hangings that leap with pattern and appear to be veritably burning up.

Bargello remains popular, not only because of its effectiveness, but also because of the speed and ease of execution. It is always satisfying to see your work developing at a rapid pace. This new free-form method adds another dimension to the kind of work that can be done in bargello.

Supplies and vocabulary

Let us consider the materials to be used. The canvas on which the stitches are worked is a mesh fabric woven of evenly spaced vertical and horizontal threads. For free-form bargello I suggest only mono canvas (woven with single threads in each direction), as opposed to penelope (woven with double threads in both directions). Interlocked canvas is also preferable since it won't unravel and stitches won't slip under intersections; traditional interwoven canvas can certainly be used, although the warp and the weft will not be of any advantage.

The gauge of the canvas is measured by the number of mesh openings between the threads in an inch. An interesting substitute for canvas, when great strength is required, is flexible fine-wire window screening from the hardware store.

Obviously, the needle is the most important tool. Keep it clean and shiny with an emery strawberry, available at any sewing or notions counter. Extra needles can conveniently be carried in your change purse, in old medicine or pill containers, or in 35-mm. film cans. The latter are best for cleanliness, but the odd needle stored in the change purse can be a real blessing if you are traveling and find yourself facing a long flight without a needle. (Incidentally, the daylight in airplanes is unusually good for doing needlework.) The size of the needle is of prime importance in relation to the gauge of the canvas. Too large a needle will distort the canvas; too small a needle will fray the wool.

Canvas Gauge	Needle
3 through 5	13
7 through 8	15 or 16
10 through 14	17, 18, or 19
16 through 18	20
20 through 32	21 through 24

Unfortunately, the trend seems to be toward importing only the even-numbered needles, leaving a serious gap, in my estimation.

A thimble is absolutely necessary and its use becomes pure habit, although it is one that people tend to fight until fingers are sore beyond belief. A tailor's thimble, open at both ends, may be the answer for anyone bothered when long fingernails hit the inside of a normal thimble. The opening in the end allows the nail to protrude.

The object in free-form bargello, as in other needlepoint, is to cover the canvas adequately and completely, without so much bulk that it is hard to pull needle and wool through the holes. Since every stitcher's tension is different, there are guidelines to be given, but common sense must prevail if the suggestions do not seem to be working for you in execution. Because it allows for flexibility, I think Persian wool is most satisfactory. The normal three-ply can easily be expanded to four- or even five-ply, or decreased to two-ply, as the situation warrants. The manner in which the wool accepts the dye can also change the ply needed to cover the canvas. A piece may be worked entirely in three-ply except for one color that requires four-ply. The darkest shades may require more strands, since you will be working on unpainted canvas and the white must not show through.

One important difference between Persian wool and knitting wool, and the reason for the former's higher cost, is that each strand of Persian wool must withstand the abrasive qualities of the canvas many times; in knitting the stress occurs only for each individual stitch, then is moved along the piece of wool as the ensuing stitches are executed.

Persian wool has "right" and "wrong" or rough and smooth directions. Always use the thread in the smooth direction. Determine this by running your thumb and forefinger down the yarn both ways. One direction should feel rougher, as if you are going against the grain. If you are unable to determine the right direction, try running the thread lightly against your upper lip; you will quickly discern the difference. If the wool is used in a longer-than-usual strand and folded in half through the needle, half of it runs in the wrong direction.

Try to make the thread lie flat and untwisted. There is no substitute for experience, but if you find that your yarn is twisting and not covering the canvas well, perhaps you need an extra ply.

The essence of any bargello is its smooth, flat effect. There is no question that frames help achieve a flatter stitch, with all threads lying smoothly next to one another, rather than twisted. Twisting of the yarn on the backside of the canvas determines the pull and position of the thread on the front. Carelessness becomes very apparent as the piece grows, and unwanted irregularities will catch the eye. A frame allows you to have both hands free so you can untwist the wool when necessary with the free hand that would otherwise be holding the canvas. For the veteran stitcher it will take some practice to work up to normal speed using a frame, but it is worth slowing down a little if the finished product is better. You will establish a rhythm once you become accustomed to the frame—the right hand accepting the needle on the backside, then returning it through the canvas to the left hand on the front. (Reverse for a left-handed person.) This allows the eye to help the less dexterous left hand. When you first use a frame, it might help to sit at a table, leaning the frame against it, unless you have a frame stand.

Be patient and you will be happy with the results. It is especially useful to work with silks or metallics on a frame, because blocking is then virtually unnecessary. Silks and metallics do need extra care when moisture is applied; refer to the chapter on blocking for details.

The use of linen, silk, and metallic threads can be very effective if not overdone. They add an extra dimension and are especially good for highlights or a change in texture.

Linen seems to improve and develop a nice sheen after it has been stitched—truly improving with age, just as old linen sheets have a luxurious quality while new ones feel as rough as muslin. The colors in linen are not extensive, but they are beautifully clear and quite different but complementary to those available in wool. Linen comes in three weights and is distinguished by numbers:

10/5	for No. 10 canvas
10/2	for No. 14 canvas
20/2	for No. 18 canvas

Again, use common sense and adjust strands to your individual tension. Test on a small square to make sure the gauge is right. If the thread does not cover properly, consider changing the size of the canvas.

Silk is very expensive and difficult to work with; it must be laid flat with each stitch to be effective. The beautiful French *Au Vers à Soie* seems superior to other brands. It is seven-stranded and strong enough to withstand the abrasion of the canvas. The elegant, lustrous, polished look may outweigh the difficulty of working with it.

DMC embroidery cotton has a brilliant range of shiny colors and is far less expensive than silk, with a similar sheen. It can be used interchangeably with silk and can produce almost the same effect. Care should be taken that all strands are separated and then combined before stitching, so threads are not twisted as they lie on the canvas. This may seem to be a real nuisance, but it is entirely necessary.

Metallic threads are surely the devil's invention, but they can add such glorious touches that we must learn to cope. Always break and never cut the desired length, preferably short, and reinforce it with a touch of white glue or clear nail polish on each end to guard against unraveling. Do ten or twelve strands at a time and let them dry before working with them. Beeswax can help if applied to the strands, and candle wax can be substituted if necessary. When fastening off metallic threads, interweave them carefully on the backside of the canvas, then reverse the direction of the interweaving for added security.

I hope we are speaking the same "language," but in order to avoid confusion I would like to define several terms used throughout the book.

Intersection is the cross formed where one vertical thread of canvas crosses one horizontal thread.

Waste stitch is used for starting work. Knot the end of the strand and insert the needle from the right side of the canvas about 2 inches away from the proposed stitches. Place the strand so the first few stitches will catch its "tail" as they are worked. These will anchor the strand. When secure the knot may be cut off, leaving no loose ends showing.

Bargello tuck is useful to finish off each strand after it has been stitched. Stop about 3 inches from the end of the strand and run it under the back of the last five or six stitches, then loop it back over one stitch and continue in the same direction under five more stitches. The loop will act as a knot without being bumpy or causing a lump. The end can be cut off and the back will stay neat and tidy. Always keep the back trimmed as you work or the ends will slip through to the front and make your work appear fuzzy.

Compensate is a word that crops up often. It refers

primarily to the stitches used in areas where there are fewer than four threads to cover and you are forced to make stitches covering either two or three threads. It will not be obvious to the beholder that you have changed the pattern unless you cover only one thread. Compensating rows are those in which the original pattern changes. To quote Marion Scoular, "Compensation stitches are partial stitches of a pattern which are used when an obstacle such as an outline or another shape interrupts the symmetry of the stitch." In project 1 the first compensating row is the fifth row stitched.

The graphs included in the following pages can be used to duplicate the pillows (Plates 1 to 12) and the spectrum (Plate 13). For the neophyte who has never worked from a graph, the illustration on page 31 should help; it indicates how the actual stitching should look after executing the graphs. Each square of the graph equals a thread of the canvas. Each symbol indicates a color change.

Color and movement

Color has been described as a phenomenon of light that enables one to differentiate otherwise identical objects. What a dismal world it would be if that were its only purpose! While color is an area within which there are ambiguities and variations in perception, it can't help but provide a tremendous source of pleasure (or dismay) to each of us in a very personal way. The more you use color, the easier it will be for you to know what combinations please or displease. Experimentation is the only way to eliminate using the same palette in everything you do. Perhaps you will keep returning to your favorite combinations, but be brave and adventuresome and try to investigate and probe. Exciting blends are sure to result.

In needlepoint we do not have the freedom to mix and make our own colors as an artist does with paints. Sometimes this can be frustrating, but the more you understand about color, the easier it will be to surmount hurdles. As you probably know, the *primary* colors are red, blue, and yellow. Their presence is strong and true, never achieved by anything but their prime existence; no other colors can be mixed to arrive at them. They are as precise as the absolute chemical elements. Certain combinations of the primary colors make *secondary* colors: red and yellow make orange; blue and red make violet; and yellow and blue make green. Two secondary colors make a pleasing combination with one primary. Now we begin to get into a more

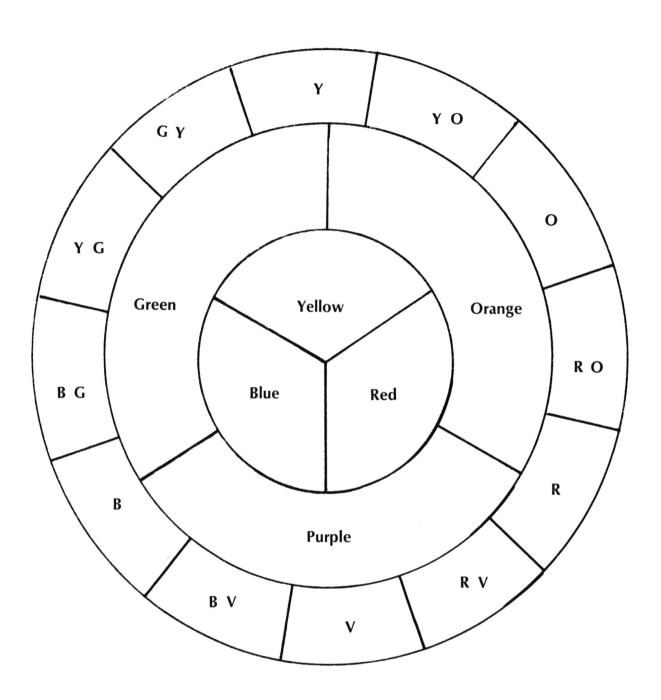

technical area which requires consulting a color wheel to simplify your understanding. *Intermediate* colors are obtained by mixing adjoining primary and secondary colors: green and blue will make turquoise, purple and red will make violet, red and orange make scarlet. *Tertiary* colors are mixed from secondary colors.

Complementary color schemes are easy to determine since you merely combine the colors directly opposite each other on the color wheel: blue and orange, red and green. The combination will be more effective if primary colors are softened and possibly divided with other neutral shades or black or white.

Analogous color schemes call for a primary color used in conjunction with colors alongside it on the color wheel. To retain continuity, the number of colors should be carefully controlled.

Monochromatic color schemes can be very effective and dramatic. Many shades of one color can be combined. If more shades are desired, wool can be split and combined with another strand as close to its shade as possible. The addition of an accent color or black or white will add dash or drama.

Hue means color saturation as opposed to mixture with black or white. When white is added to a hue, a *tint* is created. When black is added, a *tone* results. *Shades* are born from the old mixture of grays to a hue.

Value describes a color in relation to white and black—in gradations from light to dark. The addition of white results in an increase in value. If black is added, the value is lowered. Value is extremely important in developing pleasing combinations of color and, interestingly, it is most easily understood when a group of colors is transposed to a black and white photograph. When colors are similar in value but different in hue, they will still blend nicely. (As mentioned earlier, interesting effects can be obtained by combining yarns.) If these were photographed in black and white, they would appear to be one color.

The most important element is the combination of colors and how radically the whole feeling of a canvas can change as colors are moved or separated. White will always sharpen and deepen adjoining colors, while black is likely to add heaviness. I prefer to lean toward charcoal or darkest brown or bottle green when very dark effects are desired. It is more effective in wool if there is a slight cast of color. Always check colors in artificial light as well as daylight, for changes can be very abrupt and disappointing.

Colors can be neutralized when combined with others too closely related. Naturally, there will be times when this is desirable, especially in heavily shaded work.

If this all sounds too technical, don't panic. Put your color wheel away and return to your own preferences and good taste. Instinct should always be part of color choice, and many rules were made to be broken. Never let mechanical and technical methods destroy the sheer joy of creation and the fun of needlepoint. Freedom is particularly important in this new method of bargello. There is no such thing as the institutionalization of color, any more than there should be with free stitchery.

Naturally, individual tastes vary tremendously. Colors may be gaudy or tender, primary or neutral, evoking completely different reactions. A certain combination may cause anything from mild pleasure to fierce joy to sheer distaste. The safe umbrella of neutrals can generate comfort, but you should not always seek the cover of safety. Everyone prefers to work on colors that are personally pleasing and flattering, but that should not preclude the introduction of colors that might be foreign at first, but agreeable and exciting, if only because of their newness. Interestingly, the most vibrant, intense colors can be neutralized if combined with others of equal intensity, and sometimes a substitution or elimination is in order. Clear, bright colors can appear to be in motion if they are in the proper order.

Pale tones tend to show texture and movement to greatest advantage. Plate 11 in pale monochromes is a good example of movement in comparison to Plate 9, in which the darker shades tend to slow it down. Light colors seem to come forward while darker ones recede.

Although psychologists have plunged into the strange complexities regarding the pace of music heard and efficiency of production in factories and offices, few have researched the effects of colors on humans beyond the effects of "hot" colors (red, oranges, purples, fuchsias) and "cold" colors (blues, greens, mauves, turquoise, kelly, mint). Interpretation of color theory is made more difficult by its very subjective nature. One's own coloring often affects the colors that appeal and soothe. A fair-haired, blue-eyed person will most often choose pastels, blues, greens, and soft but clear colors, whereas a brunette will lean toward oranges, golds, reds, browns—all bold and strong, no matter what the personality may be.

If you stand in an orchard
In the middle of Spring
And you don't make a sound
You can hear pink sing

♦ ♦ ♦

You can smell white
In a country room
Toward the end of May
In the cherry bloom

♦ ♦ ♦

Content is gray
And sleepiness, too
They wear gray suede gloves
When they're touching you

♦ ♦ ♦

Brown is a feeling
You get inside
When wondering makes
Your mind grow wide

♦ ♦ ♦

The purple sound
Is the loveliest thing
It's the violet opening
In the spring

♦ ♦ ♦

Gold is the sunshine
Light and thin
Warm as a muffin
On your skin

♦ ♦ ♦

Green is a coolness
You get in the shade
Of the tall old woods
Where the moss is made

From "Hailstones and Halibut Bones" by Mary O'Neill

Free-form approach

I hope that by now you are curious, restless with reading, and eager to stitch. Good! For the first project, bind a 20-inch square of No. 14 canvas, preferably interlocked. Remembering that you will strive to cover four threads of canvas with each vertical stitch as often as possible, use three-ply Persian wool. Choose eight colors or shades that make a pleasing combination and place them in the order in which you expect to use them. Using pressure-sensitive labels or tags, mark each color with a number from 1 to 8, starting with the color to be used in the center, which may be a repeat of a color on an outside edge. A plastic or wooden yarn caddy can help to keep the order straight. Plastic holders for a six-pack serve equally well.

Beginning with color 2, stitch the irregular shape in Graph 1, placing it as close to the center of your canvas as your eye can judge (see pages 30 and 31). Each stitch will cover four threads, as there are no compensating stitches necessary in this row. Following the same pattern, stitch two more complete rows inside row 1, and one complete row outside row 1, all in the same color. Always stitch from blank canvas into a finished stitch, starting at one side of the pattern—the right side if you are right-handed, the left side if you are left-handed. When you have gone halfway around the pattern, turn the canvas upside down to complete the row. When compensating stitches are necessary, cover two or three threads rather than five. Never cover

29

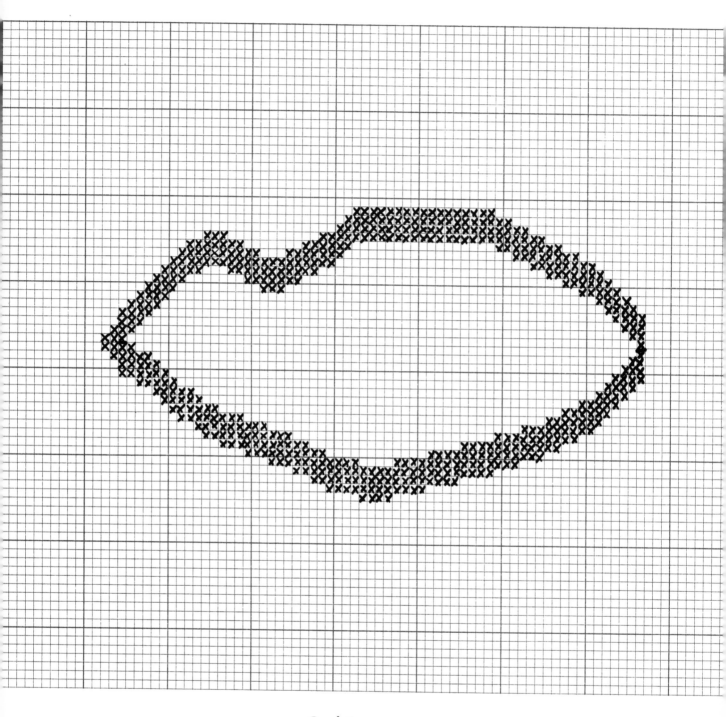

Graph 1

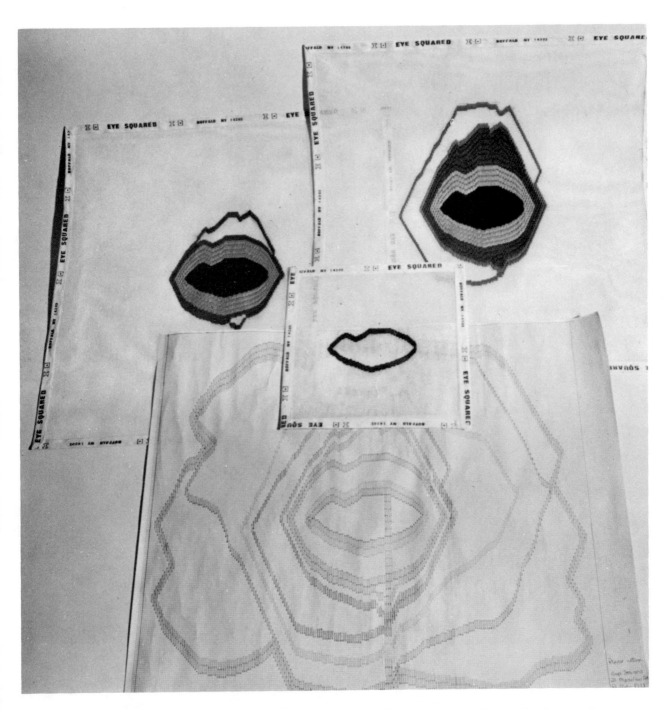

These three canvases may help the uninitiated graph reader to understand what each step should look like after stitching. The bottom graph shows all pattern changes for Project 1. See pages 34 and 35.

This enlarged graph for the first step in Project 1 should be helpful in starting the first row. On the graph the circle or dot at the base of each stitch designates the hole in the canvas where the needle enters from the back to the front. The wool thread then covers four threads of the canvas and returns to the back of the canvas at the point marked with a slash. In the foreground are two finished examples of Project 1, made up into 16-inch square pillows.

only one thread, as attention will be immediately drawn to that spot and it will appear to be a flaw.

The next inner and outer rows will be worked in a

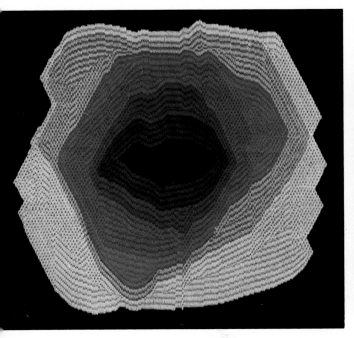

Plate 1   Free-form Project 1 in pinks, reds, and black

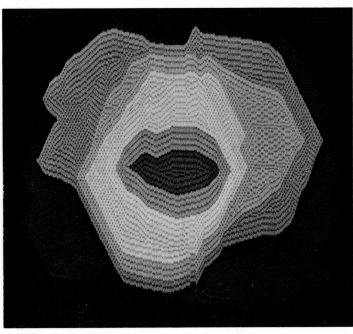

Plate 3   Project 1 in pinks and greens

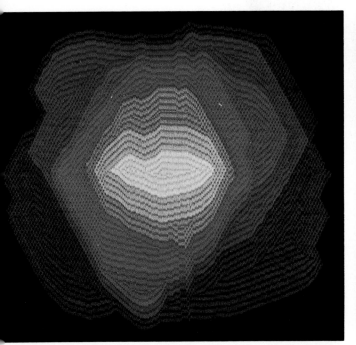

Plate 2   Free-form Project 1 in pinks, reds, and black

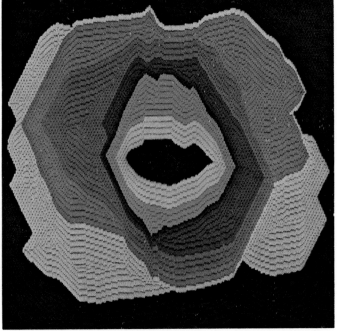

Plate 4   Project 1 in bottle green, rust, and turquoise

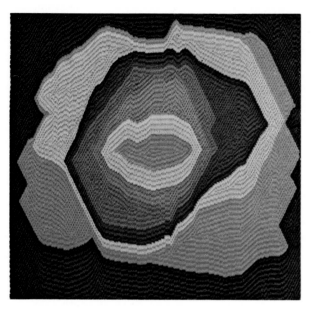

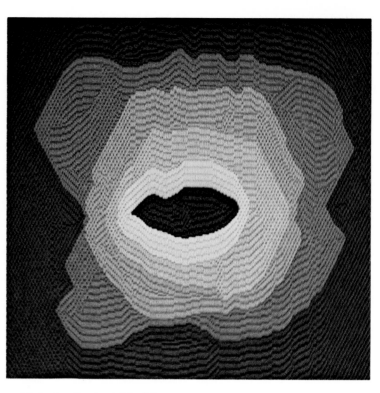

Plate 5　Project 1 in bottle green, rust, and turquoise

Plate 6　Project 1 in blues

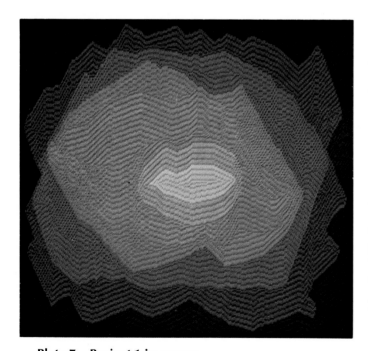

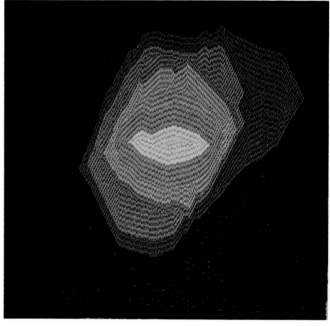

Plate 7　Project 1 in greens

Plate 8　Project 1 in browns

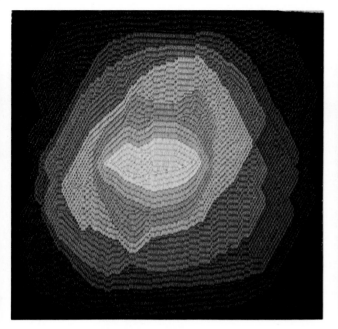

Plate 9   Project 1 in browns

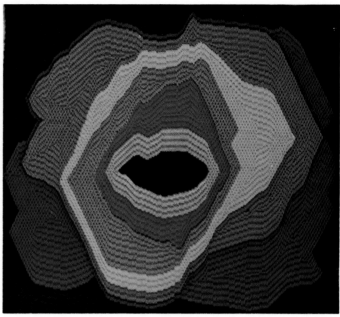

Plate 10   Project 1 in multicolor

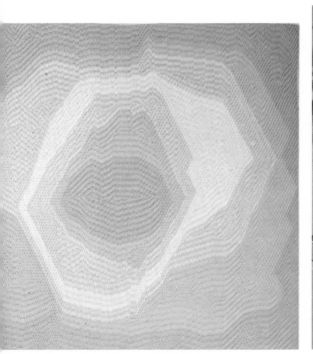

Plate 11   Project 1 in yellows

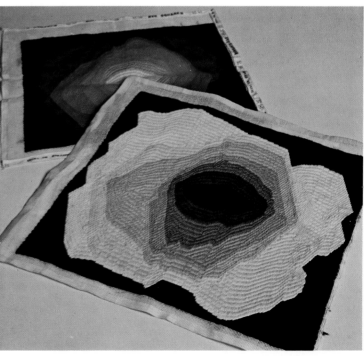

Plate 12   Project 1 in white, beige, and dark brown

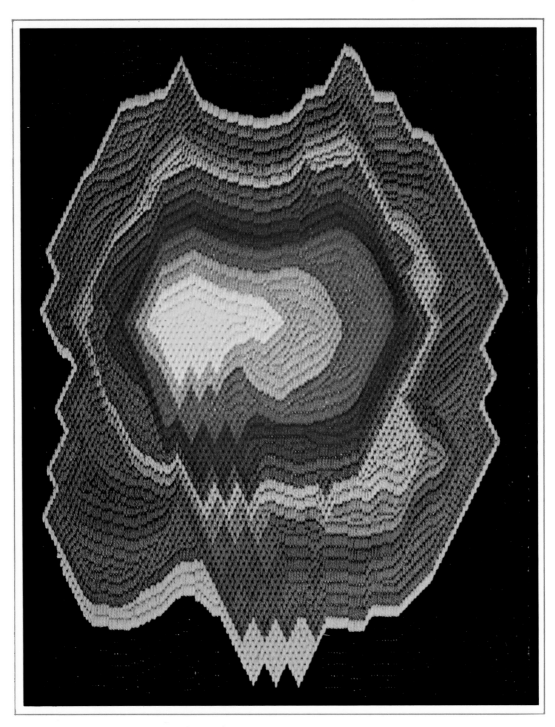

Plate 13   The spectrum (framed), Project 2

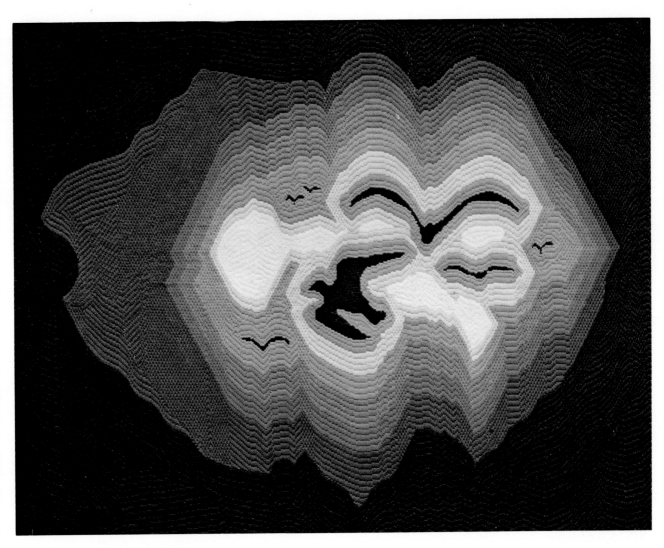

Plate 14   Sea gulls in flight

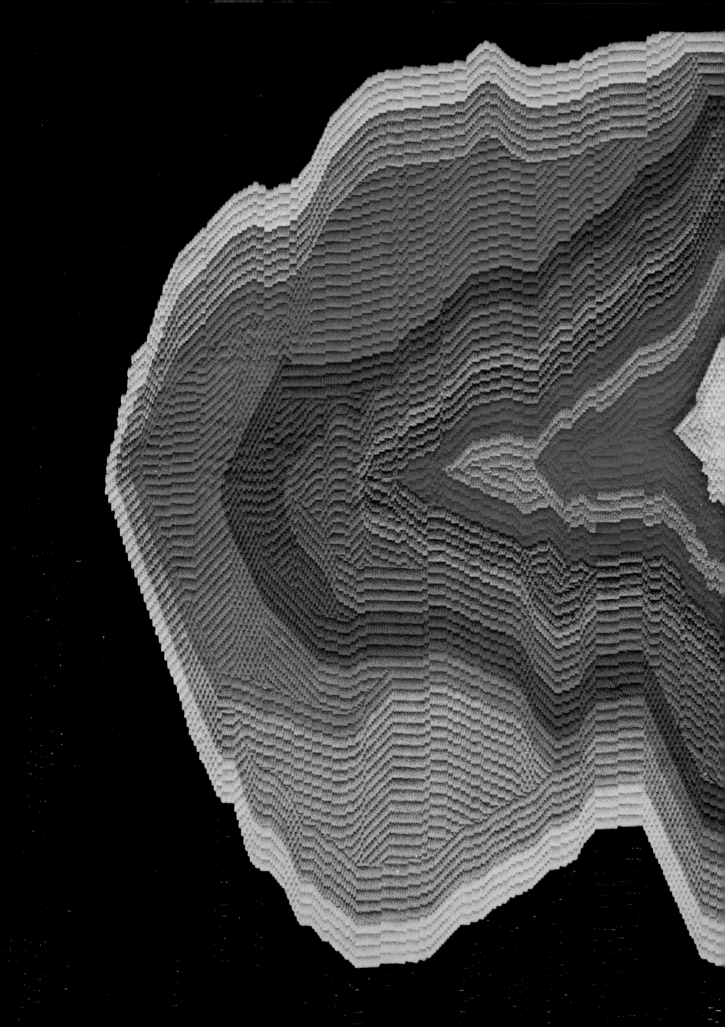

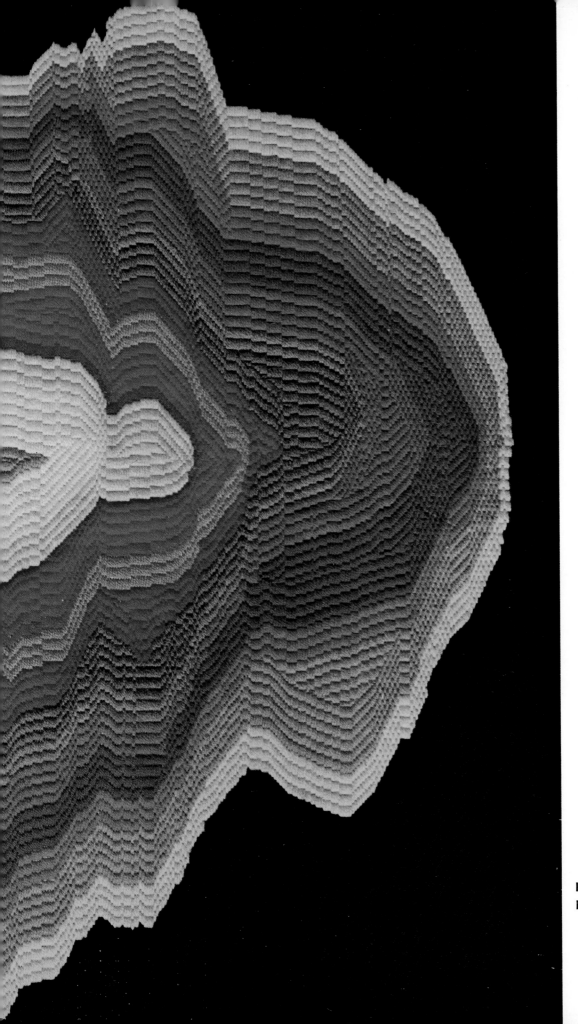

Plate 15
Free-form rug

Plate 16 Free-form wall hanging in white, beiges, and black

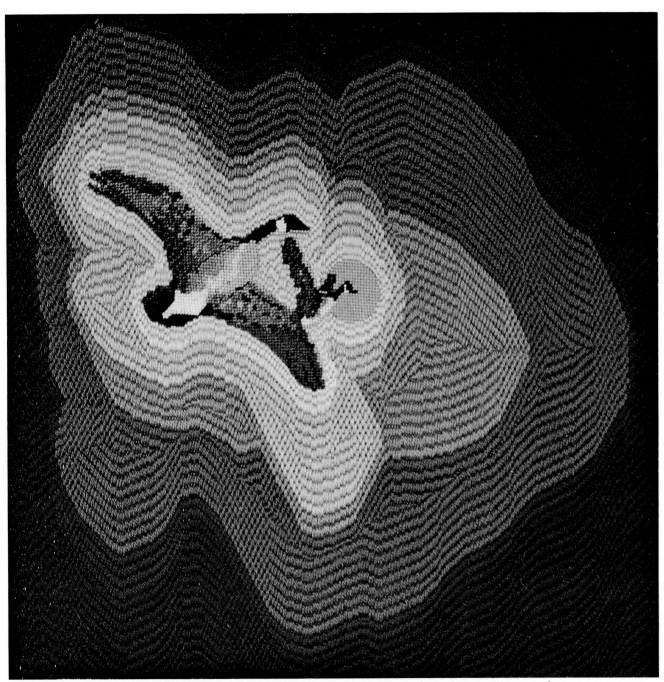

Plate 17   Canada geese in flight

Plate 18   Zebra head

Plate 19   Quadstar

Plate 20 Seashell rug

Plate 21   Blue turtle

Plate 22   Red, pink, and black
pillow on zebra
print

Plate 23   Bleeding heart on
zebra print with
heart sculpture

Plate 24   Yellow free-form pillow in yellow room

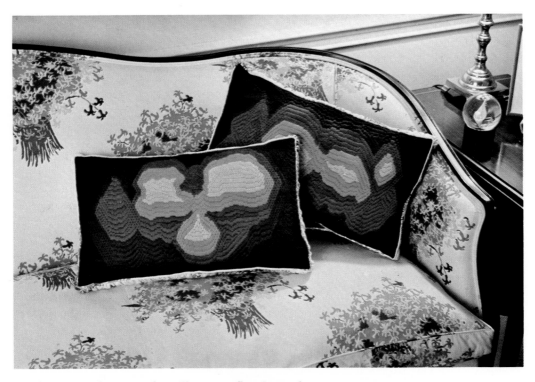

Plate 25   Blue amoeba pillows on floral couch

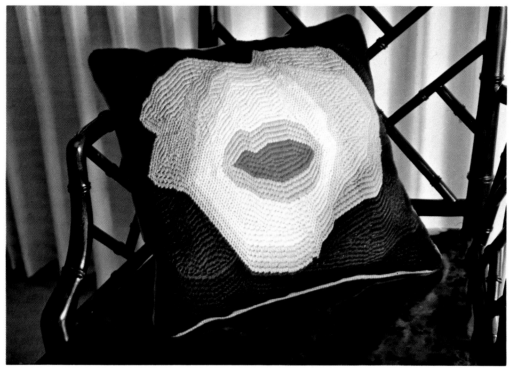

Plate 26　Pink and green free form on lattice chair

Plate 27　Free form on orange-checked couch with Chinese horse sculpture

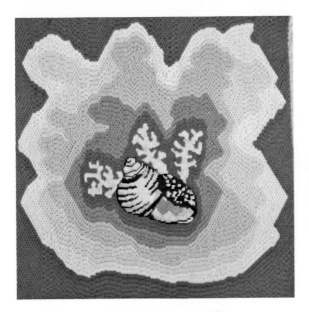

Plate 28   Seashell and coral pillow

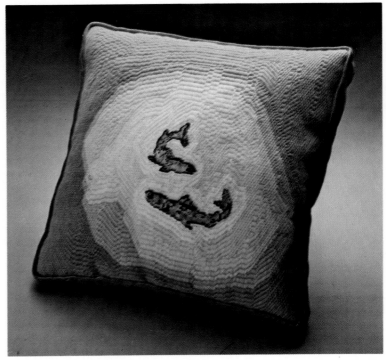

Plate 30   Two fish on free-form pillow

Plate 29   Shark's jaws

Plate 31   Rugs, pillows, and wool

different color. The inner hole can be filled in with rows covering four threads with color 1, following the pattern.

Color 3 will be introduced in the next outside row, the first compensating row of the pattern, in which a whole new pattern will be established (Graph 2; see pages 34 and 35). Follow the graph which will break off from the old pattern, leaving spaces of canvas to be filled in after the row is completed, again with rows covering four threads. When filling in the areas of blank canvas, you have three choices: (a) working around the area, in which case the effect will be like a whirlpool; (b) working the top pattern from top right to left; or (c) working the bottom pattern, right to left. These last two methods will make the piece more crisp and less flowing (see Plates 1 to 12). After blank areas are filled, stitch three more rows in the same color, following the new pattern. Now change to color 4 and stitch one row *before* the graphed compensating row, followed by one more row in the same color.

Change to color 5, stitch one row around, and then do the graphed new pattern row.

As your work develops, notice how different areas flow into each other.

Change to color 6 after filling holes made from the new pattern, with rows covering four threads, whenever possible.

Use the same method to add color 7. After filling in the complete area designated for color 7, use a *waterproof* marker (such as Nepo or Sanford Sharpie) to mark a square edge outside your free form. Your final color will follow the pattern of color 7, continuing to work around and around, stopping at the marker line which designates the outer edge. This will make a 16-inch pillow or wall hanging. It would also be a spectacular top for one of the popular Parsons tables.

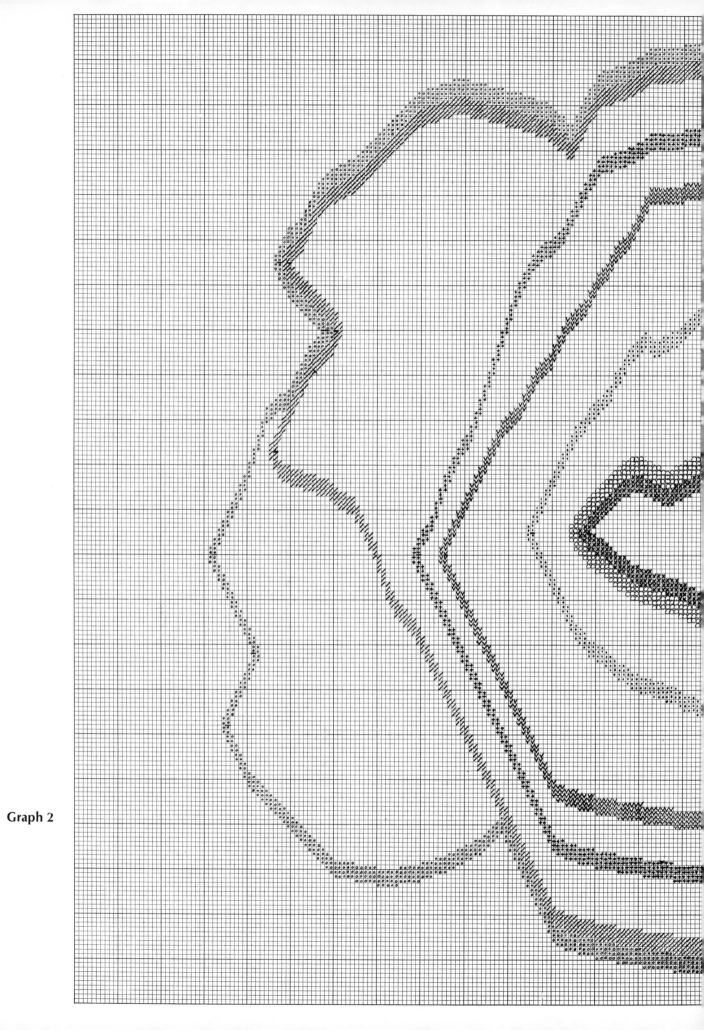

Graph 2

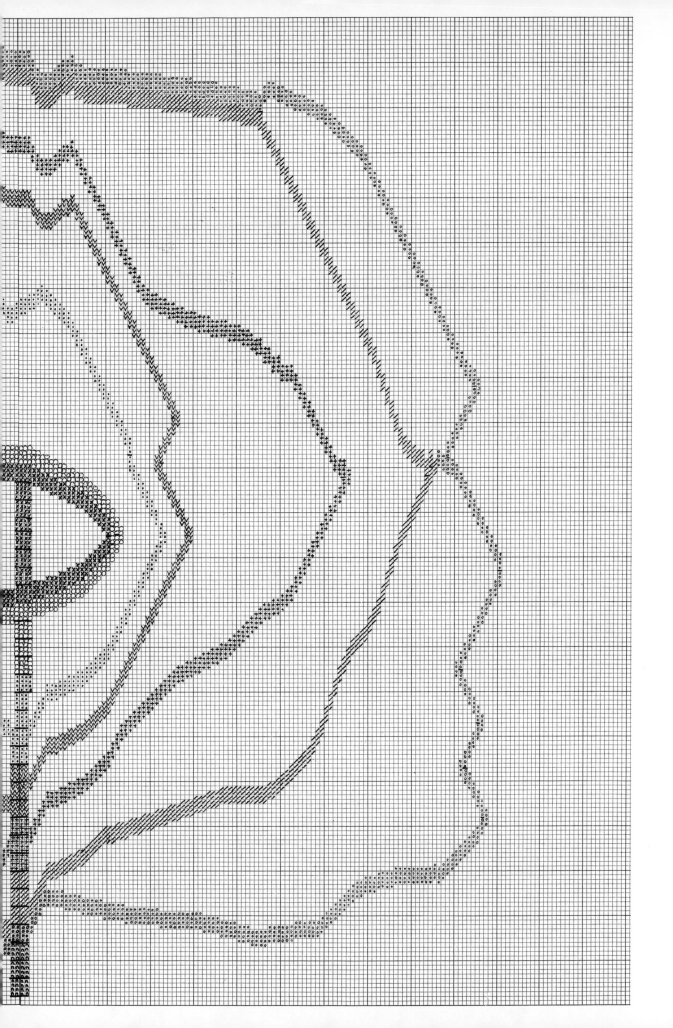

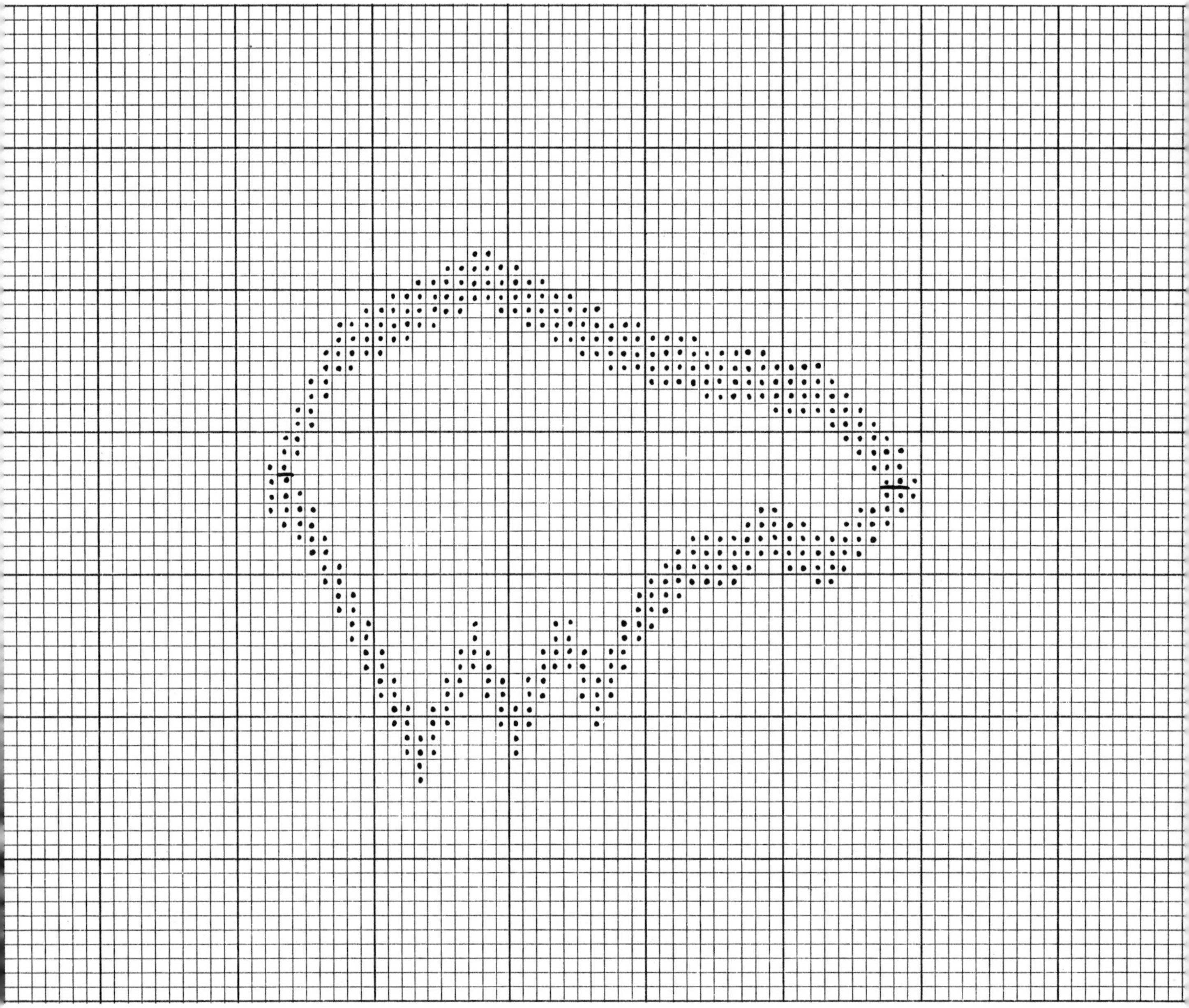

Graph 3

The graph that begins the spectrum (Plate 13) is Graph 3, which begins with the second color from the center (see photo). After stitching the one row on the graph, stitch a second row inside the first, using the same color. Again working toward the

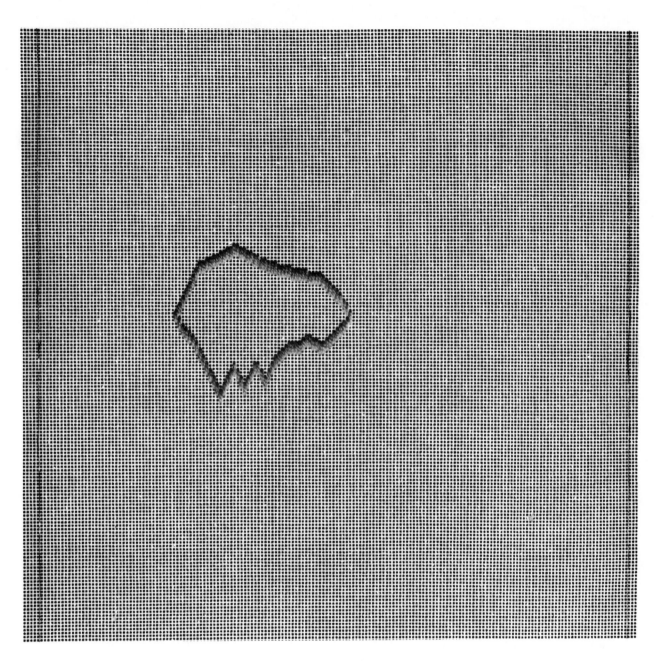

This stitched sample matches the graph for the first row of the spectrum Project 2. See pages 40 and 41 and Plate 13. Each stitch covers four threads. The jagged edges of the pattern are on the bottom part of the canvas. It is often helpful to mark the top of the canvas when you begin.

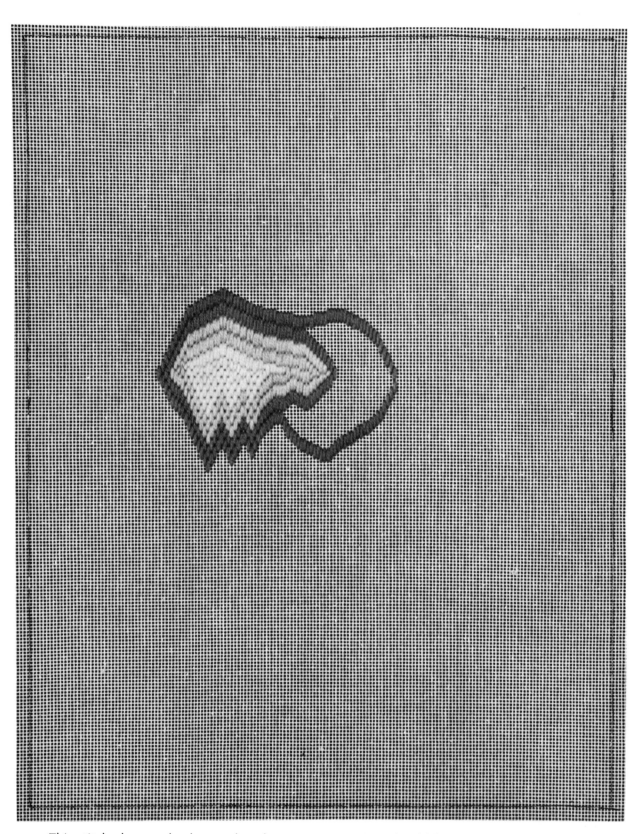

This stitched example shows what the spectrum project should look like after the third pattern change and color have been introduced.

center, stitch the next row in color 1, always covering four threads with each vertical stitch. Continue in this manner until the center area is completed. Change to color 3; do the bordering row outside the initial row. This is followed by a compensating row in the same color, read from Graph 4. Fill in the areas left blank by the pattern change, using color 3. Change to color 4 and stitch the next pattern change on the graph. As each new color is introduced, so also is a pattern change (see pages 40 and 41). Fill in blank areas formed by each change, always covering four threads whenever possible. Continue in this manner until all pattern changes have been completed. Then mark the borders for a rectangular outer edge. The last area can be filled with the same stitch or with the basket weave, if the added emphasis that a texture change makes would create a desired effect. The stitched example of Graph 4 (see page 40) indicates the vacant areas to be filled with the color on the outside of each empty area.

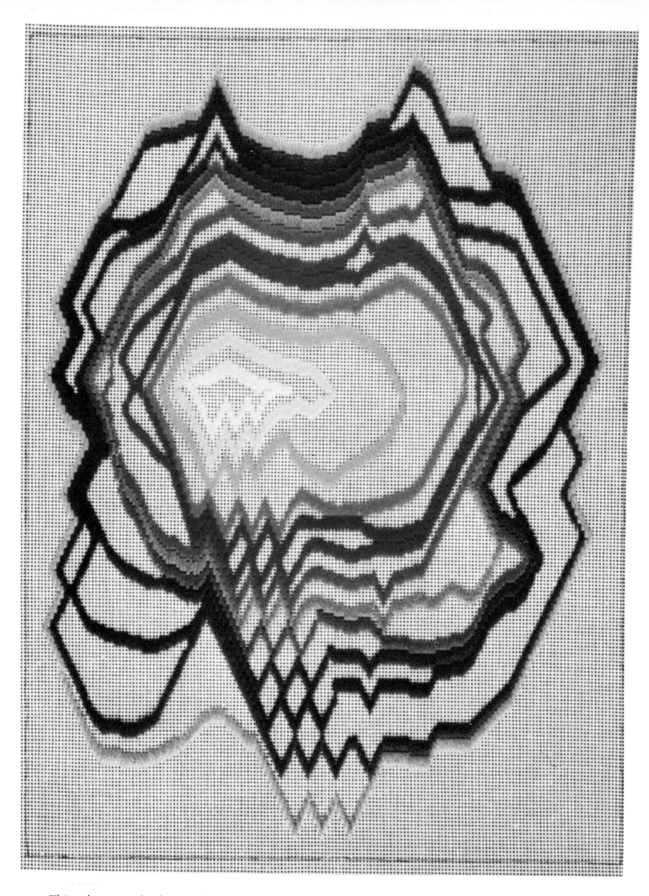

This photograph shows the spectrum with each pattern change stitched. Note that the only section that touches the previous pattern, without exception, occurs in the lower left (inverted V). This is a good point to check after each new color and pattern change have been introduced.

Graph 4

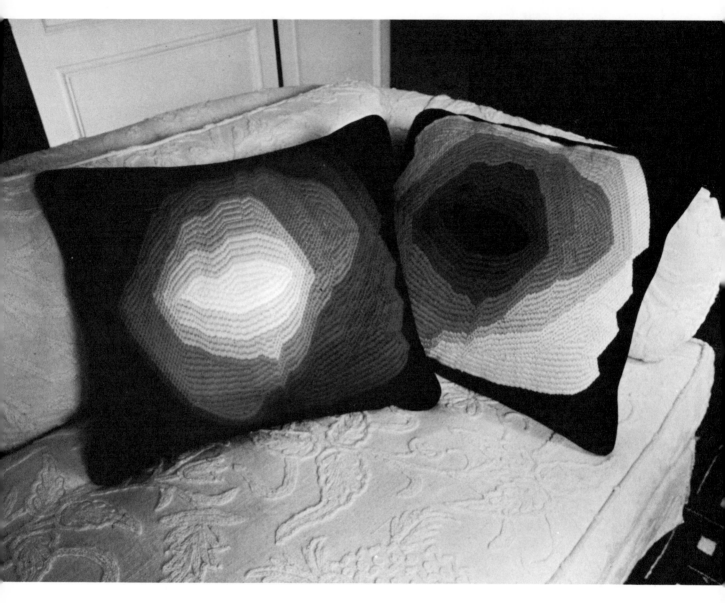

Rather than doing a pair of identical pillows, the same colors and pattern changes were used in both, but the order of shades used is different. The two designs complement each other well. Another approach might have been to use the graph in a "flop-over" or mirror image for the second pillow.

The two free-form bargello pillows in shades
of pinks and reds flowing into deep shades and then
dramatically into black illustrate how the order
of color changes the end result, even when the exact
pattern has been repeated but the colors have been
used in a different sequence (see Plate 22). How
comfortably they rest on the zebra material without
the frenzy that another actual pattern might have
created! The Kachina dolls in the background and the
Hopi Indian bowl blend well—the pillows serving as
the catalyst. A far more subdued and traditional
feeling is attained using the same pillows in a
different setting, again to good advantage, on white
crewel linen, with the textures of marble and wood
merging easily.

The free-form bargello built around an asymmetrical heart (Plate 23) contains a note of whimsy. As it developed, the heart began to bleed a little. How subtly a message might be conveyed! The textures are especially pleasing; the welded sculpture of the heart was the original inspiration for the initial pattern of bargello.

The gently flowing ruffled pillow (Plate 24) enriches the circus gaiety of the room, overflowing with patterns and textures. It detracts from nothing: the flowers, paintings, colors, sculpture, or the overall happiness of the room.

The bleeding heart design shows how an original shape that is pleasing can develop into variations of the same shape, adding interest where the pattern could be dull were it a direct repeat on each additional row.

The happy mixture of the free-form pillow and an admittedly busy pattern proves how versatile this new medium can be.

The amoeba patterns (Plate 25) add a pleasant dimension to the light and airy feeling of the floral fabric on which they rest. They were mounted with the same fabric used on the ruching which forms the boxing, the welting, and the backing.

Again, using the same graph for the first project (page 34), a more traditional pillow stitched in muted and softer colors is still extremely comfortable with an intricate maze of latticed bamboo and tortoiseshell leather (Plate 26). It would enhance a country floral chintz equally well.

The two pillows in Plate 27 were stitched as a mirror repeat, or in the flop-over method. One complements the other and adds interest, rather than being an exact replica. The change in color sequence gives added impetus. A larger project might conceivably be a rug or wall hanging started with the same pattern and expanded beyond, with the stitcher creating her own scheme.

The vibrant color of the various unrelated projects (Plate 31) show the versatility of the new free-form media. Even on the small jewelry case (executed in DMC cotton floss on No. 14 canvas), the limited space still lends itself to a graceful, free design. It is equally acceptable on the large (36-inch-by-50-inch) wall hanging or rug, although perhaps the use of more shades or colors on the larger projects helps to keep the viewer pleased. Boredom might be caused if there weren't a pattern change with each color change. For the beginner, the "middle-of-the-road" project, illustrated by the five pillows (16 inches square), is the best way to become acquainted with the method. (See Graphs 1 and 2 and accompanying explanations and directions.)

The drama of the birds and swirls of the clouds and air currents is effective even in black and white. If you choose to use colors other than the turquoises (Plate 14), the gradations in this photograph should help make selection easier, without the distractions of color.

Large projects

Any of the designs in this book that were developed for pillow-size projects could be enlarged for larger ones. Free-form bargello is especially adaptable for projects like area or room-size rugs or wall hangings. It works up quickly and the movement and motion possible take some of the boredom out of stitching large areas of background. The result is far more interesting to view as well. The movement around the sea gulls (Plate 14) is created by far more than a color change. If the whole piece had been worked in basket weave, it would have lost the strong feeling of the swirls of air surrounding the sea birds, and much of its charm.

The suggested method of starting somewhere near the center of the canvas is a great advantage as the piece grows, for the hand holding the unworked canvas does not have to cope with large areas of bulky, stitched canvas. There is nothing that can alleviate the weight of a growing large project, but the problem can be slightly mitigated if a small breakfast tray with legs is placed across the lap, under the work being stitched. This is especially effective in warm climates, summertime, anywhere. It eliminates the feeling of stitching underneath a warm quilt. A standing floor frame is another solution, but it is not as portable and does require the patience of learning to work with one hand above and one below—a facility worth acquiring but more sensibly begun on a smaller project.

The same delight can be found in watching a large

project develop as in working with smaller pieces. It is helpful occasionally to place the canvas on the floor and walk away from it, even to leave the room. Upon re-entering, cast a critical glance, trying to determine areas that need enlarging for balance. Sometimes it is helpful to sketch an outline with a waterproof, indelible, permanent pen in an area that appears wanting. The outline does not have to be rigidly adhered to but can act as a suggested guideline. As the drawn pattern is filled, new directions will unfold.

For a given area, it is interesting to note the choices available and the results that develop. The area rug (Plate 15) would have looked quite different if the outside black had been repeated in the center; it would have given it the eerie look of a hole.

Transferring designs
to canvas

The designs and sketches in this book are included for those who need to copy. One of the greatest advantages in using the photostat process of reproduction is that it keeps the basic proportion and design intact but eliminates minute detail. Conversely, the designs can provide a springboard for more detailed and intricate projects. All are planned in such a way that their outside edges provide the beginning of the free-form bargello. Basket weave is the desired and proposed stitch for all the initial forms, as the textural change to bargello is more effective than if coarser stitches were chosen and no shading used. The designs are also included to tempt your adventuresome spirit and inspire you to create your own. If the same size as is illustrated is desired, simply trace it onto white or tracing paper so it will be flat and easier to place under the canvas. If a size change is needed, the simplest way is to have a photostat made at any commercial photocopying store. They can enlarge or reduce to the exact size required at very reasonable fees. Order a positive print, which is easier for a beginner to work with, although perhaps not necessary as proficiency develops.

If you are using interwoven canvas, the warp threads (parallel to the selvage) must run up and down the canvas (vertical threads). In planning a design to be surrounded by free-form bargello, be very generous with the size allowance. As the free form develops, it is interesting to watch patterns evolve. The piece may cry for an explosion in one direction, unplanned at inception, and this can be satisfied only if extra canvas has been allowed. A good example is the turtle (Plate 21), stitched on a 20-inch-by-20-inch square, off-center and placed with no real size plan in mind. The same was true of the zebra (Plate 18), which was started on a 24-inch-by-28-inch canvas and allowed to grow until the proportion of the background seemed a proper balance for the basket-weave zebra head.

Prepare your canvas with masking tape or cotton binding on the edges.

The easiest way to transfer the design to the canvas is to use a real or improvised light table. To improvise, tape the design onto a glass table, and place your canvas over it so that your design shows through exactly where you want it to appear. The canvas can be taped on one side but should be loose enough to allow for peeking underneath in case the design is either not clear or particularly intricate. Place a light bulb or table lamp on the floor underneath the table. Its light should make the tracing job very simple. Be sure to use a waterproof, indelible, permanent marking pen. There are some on the market especially developed for needlepoint, and it is well worth searching them out. The newer gray ones are superior to black, as they will not show through pastel or white wool. When the whole pattern has been transferred to the canvas, a quick spray of a clear fixative is a sensible added precaution. Any art store and most hardware stores have this available in spray cans. It is also advisable to use the fixative over any color you may paint on your canvas. Artist's acrylics are the easiest to handle, with a poor second choice being artist's markers. It is not always necessary to add color to your canvas, especially if light colors are being added and there aren't many heavily shaded areas. If dark colors are being used, painting the canvas before stitching will tend to alleviate the problem of any white threads showing through. Always paint with a paler shade than the planned color of the yarn. Anyone who has ever stitched black on a black painted canvas will know how much easier on the eyes it would have been had the canvas been painted a medium gray instead.

Generally, as you become more advanced and relaxed, color can be kept at a minimum and you will derive satisfaction as the piece comes to life with the stitching rather than the painting. You should have a master plan—even if it changes drastically as the work develops. Color changes can also be made even after the painting stage. Simply use white acrylic to cover the involved areas and after it has dried reapply the new colors over the white areas. Do try, however, not to plug up the holes in the canvas. Experience will soon dictate the thickness of the paint that works best.

The canvas areas under the free-form bargello are better left unpainted, or some of the intriguing freedom of the method will be lost. If the white threads begin to show through the darker wools, simply add an extra ply of yarn, even though some of the areas have been stitched with fewer. Your goal is to cover the canvas, and if some areas require three threads and some take four, the difference will not be discernible unless the white canvas is showing and drawing unwanted attention.

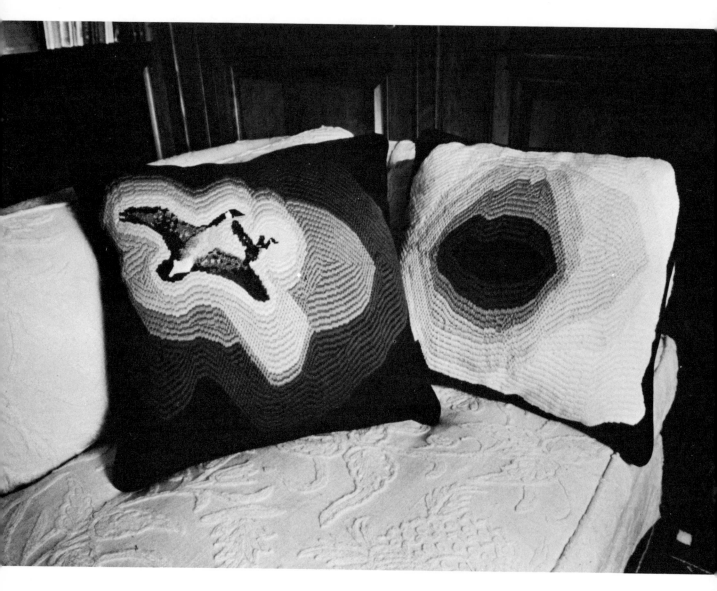

Complete balance is evident in the combination of a free-form pillow and one combining the Canada geese with a free-form background. The patterns of movement that develop are complementary rather than in opposition, even though they are dissimilar. Using the same colors on the two pillows makes the blending even more graceful, while changing the order adds interest. (One color scheme fades from light to dark, the other from dark to light.)

Design by explosion

Let us now consider the many effects that can be produced by combining free-form bargello with an area of traditional basket weave, either in silhouette or executed with meticulous detail and heavy shading. The beauty of this approach is that the outer shape of the basket-weave area provides the beginning pattern of the free-form bargello. Ensuing rows can either dramatize the shape or soften it. The colors of the free-form bargello can pick up those already used in the realistic area, or colors in direct contrast can be chosen, creating an entirely different effect.

After the realistic portion of the design has been stitched, it is advisable to surround it with one row of tent stitch in the same color as that of the first row of the background bargello. This will compensate for the sometimes ungraceful meeting of the diagonal and vertical stitches, allow for the canvas to be well covered in the intervening area, and the first bargello rows will not infringe upon the stitched design.

As a first project, something in silhouette is a good choice. Birds are effective (Plate 14), as are flowers, leaves, seashells, trees, butterflies, and bumblebees, or virtually any other form that is graceful and easily recognizable. This area should be stitched first, preferably not in the continental stitch so the shape of the canvas will be retained. Some suitable designs have been included in the chapter dealing with transferring designs to the canvas. They can be enlarged or reduced, according to the effect desired and the size of the project being undertaken.

If more than one area has been stitched in basket weave, the first color of the free-form bargello should be repeated around each figure until the areas meet (see Plate 14). Once they have met, the shape produced is the first bargello pattern. From this point outward, as a new color or shade is introduced, so should the pattern be varied to provide interest and emphasize the easy, free-flowing feeling of this method. There should be nothing stilted or stiff—even a straight black and white combination should still move freely. Two examples using the same color combination serve as illustrations of how this should be done (Plates 16 and 17). They also show how free-form bargello complements more traditional patterns.

The Canada geese pillow (Plate 17) shows the close relationship that can be developed by combining free-form bargello with a design executed in basket weave, using the outside edge as the initial pattern for the bargello. The muted colors add emphasis to the swirling air around the birds. The splash of color amplifies the drama of flight and the grace of the geese. The companion pillow fits comfortably without distracting or adding confusion, even though the pattern of the free form is completely different from all the patterns surrounding it (see page 54).

"Zebra in explosion" (Plate 18), consisting of only blacks, reds, and white, relies on the theory of motion and creates an example of the freedom that can be attained with free-form bargello.

Zebra head

Sometimes areas seem to have a mind of their own—they simply take over and the effects you had in mind seem impossible to achieve. Don't be afraid to rip; it is better than letting a poorly worked area ruin the whole piece. The quadstar (Plate 19) was such a piece for me. At first there were too many swirls in the bargello which detracted from the pure lines of the design. The easy curves that replaced whirlpools have added a nice dimension—impossible if a regular structured stitch had been used as a background. My initial plan had been to repeat the quadstar form in the background, using it to create new patterns. It didn't work.

The quadstar is actually a logo for the initials *P* and *L*, equally visible from top, sides, or up-side down. The motion in the background is subtle enough not to detract from the balance of the main design, but it still provides interest that might be lacking in a more traditional background stitch.

The seashell rug or wall hanging (Plate 20) could be done in any number of color combinations to equal advantage. For instance, by merely changing the small areas of color in the shell and then repeating these new colors in the outer bargello the piece could have quite a different effect. If a less dramatic end were sought, the use of very pale colors and a more conservative pattern change would satisfy. Using several shades of white in the explosion would put more emphasis on the pattern set by the stitches and would appear like water or wind currents. This is also true of the Canada geese (Plate 17). The soft shades convey a real feeling of the motion of flight, even more clearly emphasized when reproduced in black and white (see page 54).

The beginning rows of bargello surrounding the shaded seashell show the way the background can take its pattern from the center design. In succeeding rows the jagged edges of the shell are more dramatically emphasized, adding extra interest as the piece develops. See Plate 20.

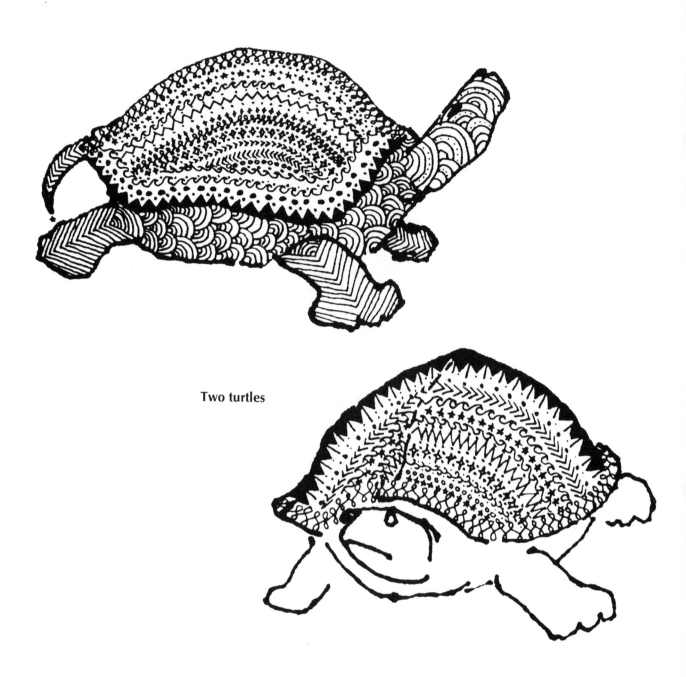

Two turtles

The turtle (Plate 21) demonstrates how surface embellishment can be attained by superimposing embroidery or crewel stitches over the worked basket weave, then surrounding it with free-form bargello. The intricate design contrasts sharply with the freedom of the other areas. It is a pleasant relief after working in the confines of petit point to be able to move on to bargello gracefully and effectively.

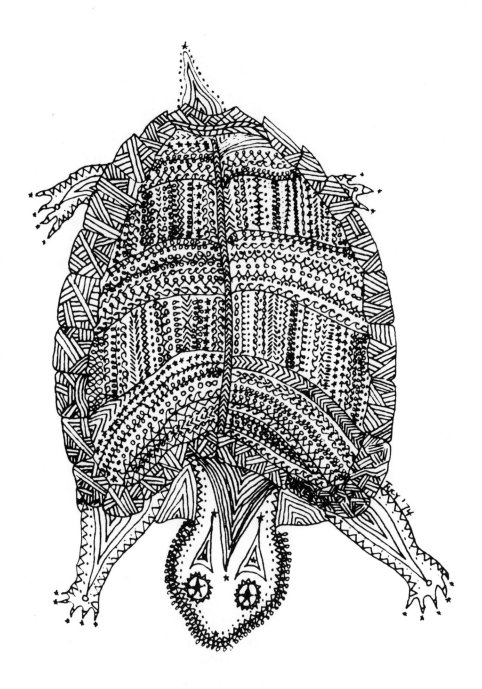

Top view of turtle

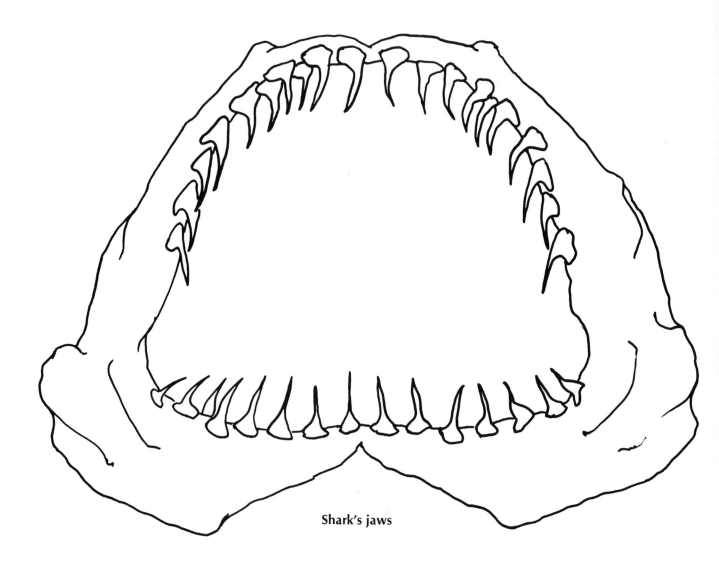

Shark's jaws

The shark's jaws (Plate 29) represented an interesting challenge. The dramatic shape of the teeth gave a thrust to the inner areas and a frothy magnification to the violence so often connected with the animal. The smooth outer edge connotes sleek and quiet movement through deep waters toward unknown depths, with the darkest shades on the outside.

The seashell and coral (Plate 28) provide an additional exercise in design. Many more pieces of coral could have been used if a more intricate pattern was desired. The delicacy achieved in this pillow was a result of the design as well as the soft palette of corals and pinks.

The dramatic shapes of the coral add an extra dimension to the seashell design, easily picked up in the background. While the stitched version (see Plate 28) is in fairly subtle shades of coral, you can imagine the very different effect it would have if more vibrant colors or shades were introduced—or the even softer effect if it were done in shades of white and gray, or in any pale monochromatic scheme.

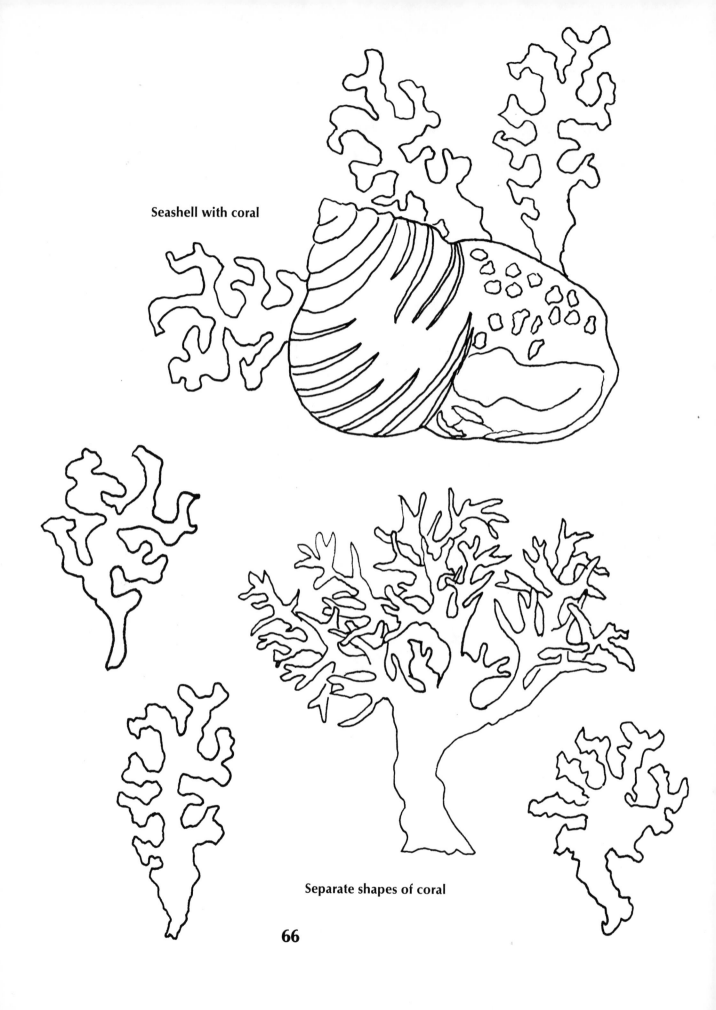

Seashell with coral

Separate shapes of coral

66

Owl

The owl would be most effective stitched in petit point in basket weave, then embellished with an overlay of embroidery stitches: spider's webs on the chest, French knots where the dots appear, and perhaps some turkey work on the brow. The more intricate the overlay, the better. Silk or embroidery floss could be used to good advantage and would help to form a dramatic contrast to the free-form bargello which will take its shape first from the outside edge of the owl and the branch.

The same approach is suggested for the next eight drawings. The intricate pattern encased in simple outer boundaries will result in spectacular projects—each one will be unique not only because the subject matter is varied, but also because each outside shape, which is the basis for the first row of the free-form bargello, is entirely different.

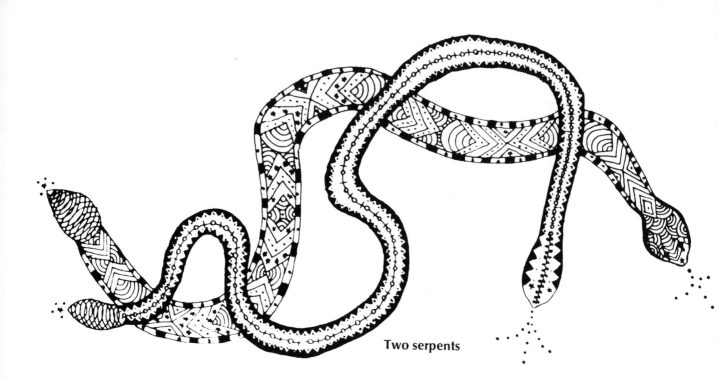

Two serpents

Candle

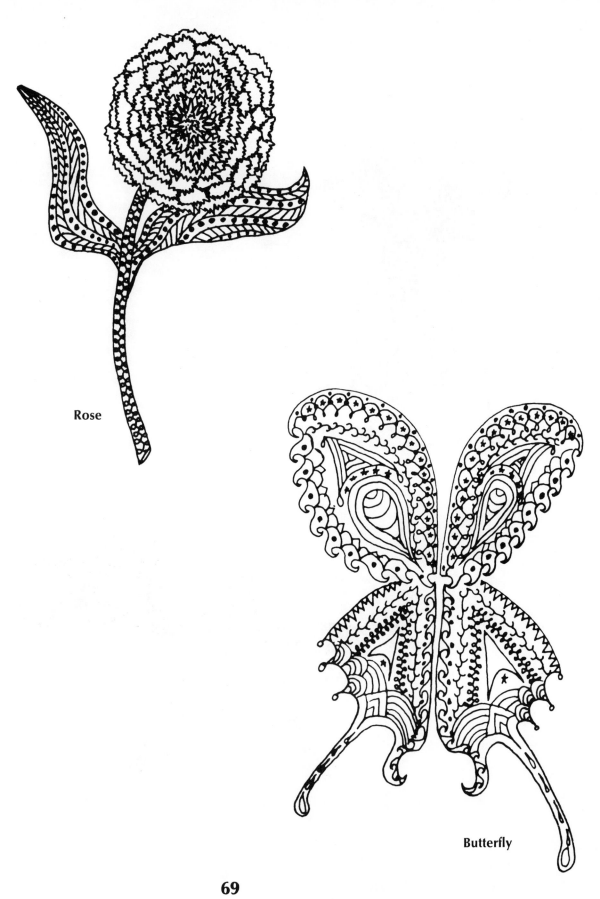

Rose

Butterfly

69

Jug of flowers

Stars

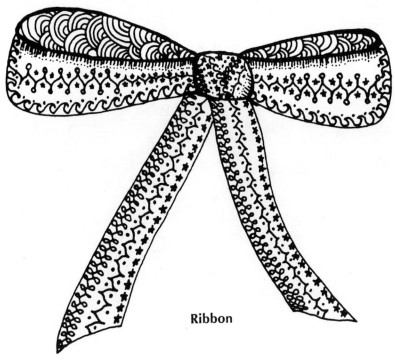

Ribbon

Mushrooms

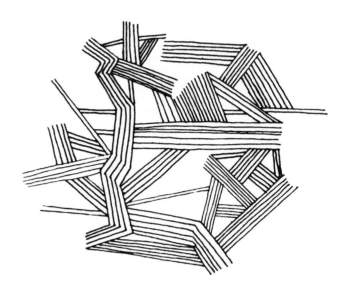

Geometric patterns

These abstract designs are easily adaptable to any color scheme imaginable. Since there are so many small areas to be stitched, they provide an excellent way to use up scraps of wool. The contrast between the straight linear patterns and the developing free form in the outer regions is fascinating.

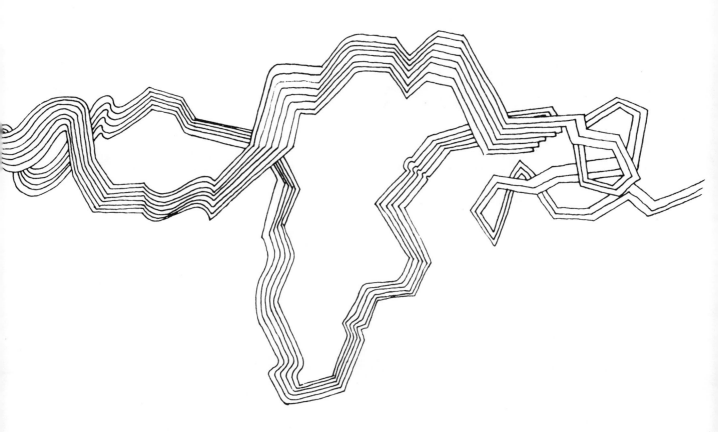

The chains should be stitched on fine canvas to achieve the desired precision of their duplication in sharp contrast to the flowing areas that surround them.

Chains

The clubs and balls would be most effective worked in black and white with the surrounding bargello relying on several shades of a single color, preferably muted.

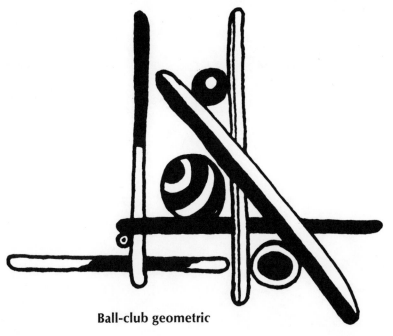

Ball-club geometric

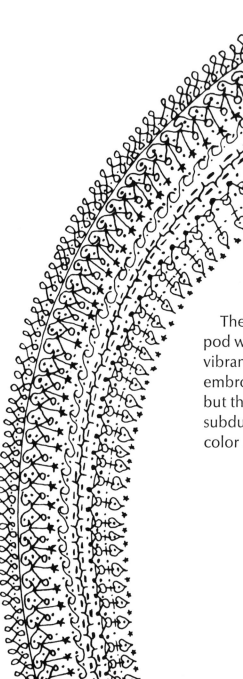

Rainbow

The "sparkler," the rainbow, and the circular seed-pod would each be most effective with the use of vibrant colors, especially in the overlay of embroidery stitches. A full spectrum could be used, but the surrounding bargello should be more subdued, relying on swirling patterns rather than color so that it won't become too busy. The

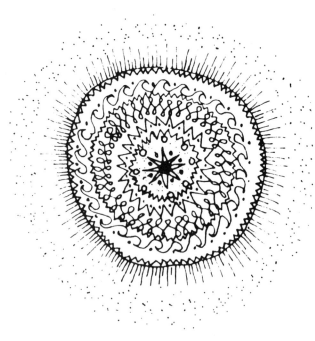

Circular seedpod

Textured ball with shadow

introduction of very textured stitches is called for in
the textured ball with shadow, and possibly the use
of metallic threads or silk. The finished work should
have a lumpy, three-dimensional appearance. The
smoothness of the surrounding bargello will be a
satisfying backdrop.

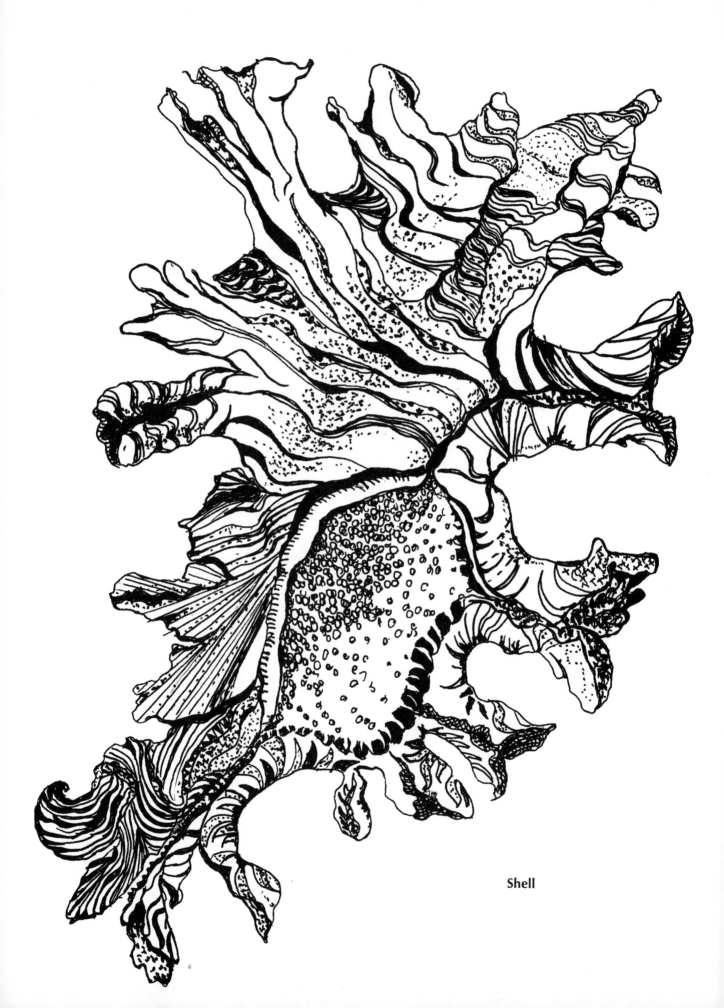

Shell

The shell is drawn in such a manner that the stitcher has several choices. Heavy shading or heavy embroidery would enhance the design, and it is equally suitable for a large or small project. Plate 20 is an area rug or wall hanging, but it could also be made into a handsome floor cushion.

The two fish gracefully complement each other as well as provide a smooth, flowing pattern for the bargello. The illusion of both water and swimming is easily achieved.

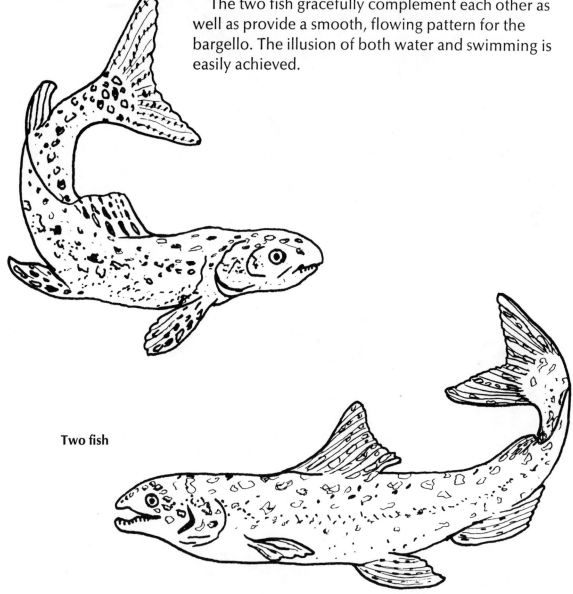

Two fish

Thorn tree

The two giraffes would be effective in a wall hanging (if enlarged) or a pillow. The surrounding areas should repeat the patterns formed by their markings.

Even without the advantage of having visited East Africa, anyone with a casual interest in wild creatures and their environment is probably familiar with the incredibly exotic flat-topped acacias, or thorn trees, scattered at random, giving welcome shelter and food to so many African animals. The thorn tree design could provide added interest if combined with the giraffes, although the superb tree can easily stand alone.

Two giraffes

The Masai tribal warriors of East Africa produce spectacular geometric patterns, used primarily on their impressive shields. Reproduced as a central theme, the different shapes could be repeated at random on the background of the canvas, each creating a pattern change of its own. These in turn would meld with the other areas as the background is completed. Traditionally the shields are painted in warm, earthy tones—reddish browns, creams, grays —blending comfortably in contrast with the drama of coal black and bright red. The designs alone are strong enough to be used with any color combination and palette, but a careful balance should be retained to remain effective.

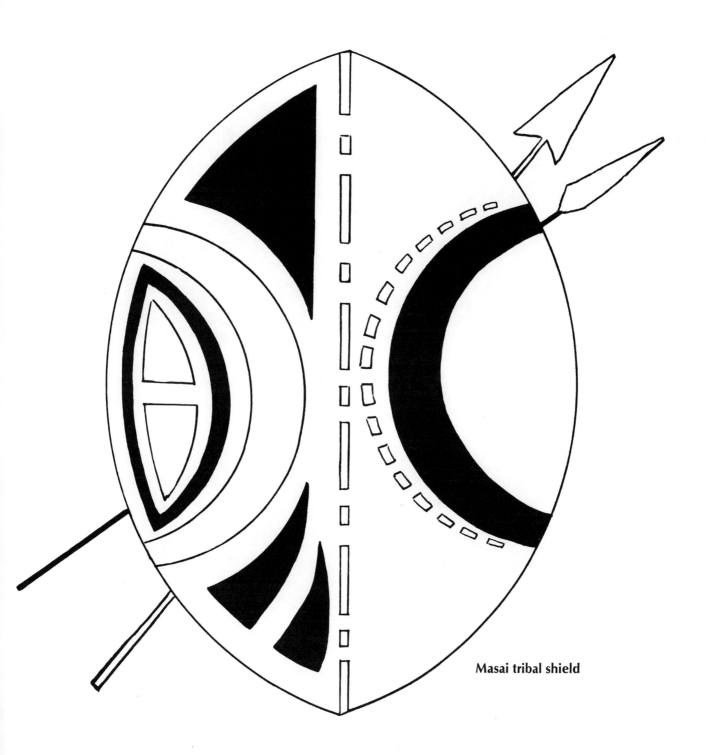

Masai tribal shield

Variation on an onion

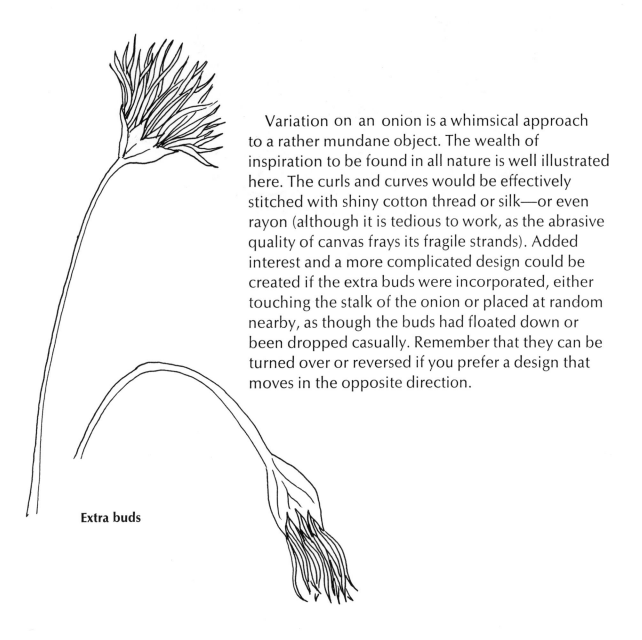

Variation on an onion is a whimsical approach to a rather mundane object. The wealth of inspiration to be found in all nature is well illustrated here. The curls and curves would be effectively stitched with shiny cotton thread or silk—or even rayon (although it is tedious to work, as the abrasive quality of canvas frays its fragile strands). Added interest and a more complicated design could be created if the extra buds were incorporated, either touching the stalk of the onion or placed at random nearby, as though the buds had floated down or been dropped casually. Remember that they can be turned over or reversed if you prefer a design that moves in the opposite direction.

Extra buds

Star flower

The star flower is a stylized design, suitable for several color approaches: bright, violent, flat colors, or a soft, muted, heavily shaded combination in pastels. The zigzag on the leaves could be stitched in basket weave with the rest of the flower, or added afterwards, with an overstitch in floss on top of the needlepoint. A dramatic effect could be achieved by adding metallic threads to the center of the flower as well.

The spiny, graceful curves of the chrysanthemum might be executed completely in satin stitch, carefully laid on fairly fine canvas, the direction of the stitch being dictated by the curve of each petal—a nice contrast to the vertical direction of the background bargello.

Chrysanthemum

Dragons and monsters and incredibly imaginative compilations of human and animal forms were all a part of olden times, helping to explain the unknown, or at least to have a surface description. Even today fantasy slips into our ordered lives, perhaps with a wee bit more humor, but with the same escapism. Inspiration can be found in many ancient civilizations, as in the early oriental periods. One example is the command bird, surely imaginary, with its unusual plumage and regal bearing. It was used as a symbol of peace and prosperity. It is easily adaptable to needlepoint and provides a pleasant relief from the traditional winged creatures. It invites clashing, vibrant use of color, as unconventional as its form.

Command bird

Also inspired by early oriental design, but expressing a far different approach, the clean, fluid lines of the floating bird would combine elegantly with free swirls of clouds in a free-form bargello background. The pattern would be drawn from the outside edge of the bird, then repeated in various areas. The floating bird would be most effective placed off center on the canvas. It is suitable for a small project but could be repeated to form an elegant rug or wall hanging.

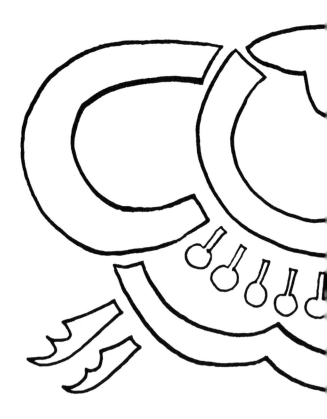

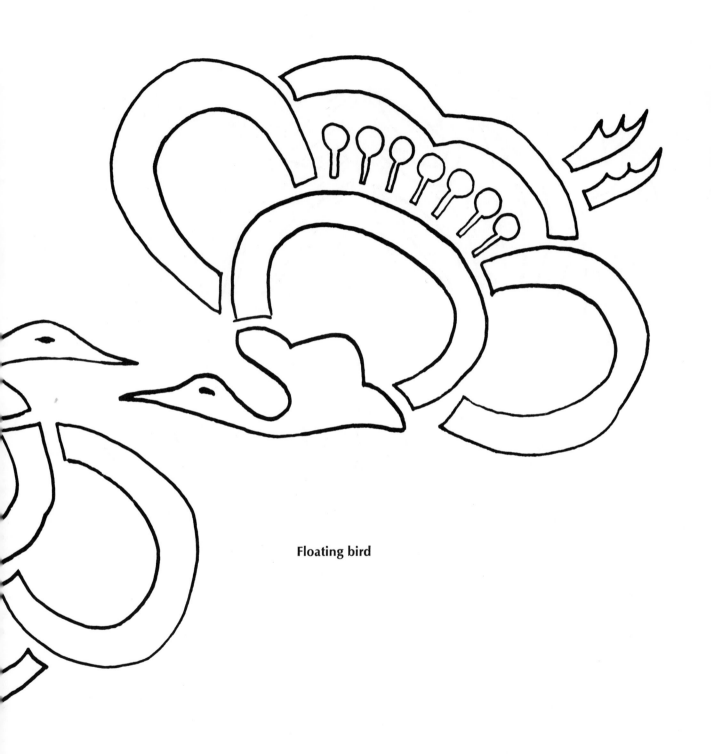

Floating bird

Gentian

Crests and badges form the basis for Japanese heraldry, developed in the tenth century. The pure, artistic lines of the patterns are so typical of the beautiful simplicity we have found the Japanese to be so capable of producing. Unlimited symbols,

Tree peony

gracefully adapted to needlepoint, can be found in a boundless range of subject matter, both imaginary and natural. The gentian and the tree peony could combine to make a stunning pair of round pillows, suitable for traditional or contemporary decor. The

Cherry blossom

cherry blossom or the plum blossom used together would provide a pleasant design suggesting a negative-positive mirror effect, without being an actual reflection. They would be very effective

Plum blossom

stitched with the same color combination but in reverse order, the color fading from light to dark on one and dark to light on the other.

Outline of sea gulls

Designing your own

As you become more accustomed to the freedom of free-form bargello, you will begin to see the possibilities for new projects in unsuspected places. If you have trouble drawing, your photocopy company can become your best friend. The sources of inspiration are endless: children's books, nature books, wallpaper, wrapping paper, fabrics, super-graphics, posters, greeting cards, magazine and newspaper illustrations, Chinese designs, Indian art books, flower catalogs, Golden Book series, post-cards (especially those from art galleries and art stores), Christmas cards, and so on. With the help of a camera, three-dimensional sculpture can offer very imaginative patterns. The camera easily does the work of reducing the sculpture to a two-dimensional surface.

Silhouettes provide great beginnings. The sea gulls in flight (Plate 14) is a good example. Cut out several of the shapes, then place them within the outline you have chosen for the size of your project. Move the figures around and remember to consider both sides, or the flop-over, as possible designs. When you think you have found a pleasing arrangement, make a tracing and then leave it for a while. It is interesting how much more objective and discerning you become after leaving the task for a short time. Asymmetry is very effective since balance can be achieved quite easily as new patterns grow in the free-form areas. If a project seems to be leaning or moving in a direction with too much force or emphasis, compensation is a simple answer. Merely enlarge the area of bargello that appears wanting. Once you have decided on the placement, a light table is the ideal way to transfer the design to canvas; although with bold silhouettes, it is fairly easy to lay the piece of canvas over the design and outline it directly. Be absolutely certain to use a waterproof pen such as a Nepo marker, made primarily for needlepoint. I prefer a gray marker to black. If mistakes are made as you are drawing on the canvas, use white acrylic artist's paint to cover them.

If you are working from a photocopy, first transfer the design to tracing paper. If you have a glass-top table, simply place a lamp underneath it on the floor. Place the canvas over the design on the table and transfer it. If such an arrangement is not available, taping the canvas over the design to a window with masking tape will work well, although it is a strain on the arm muscles. If fairly coarse canvas is being used (No. 10 or No. 12), it may be possible to trace the design without extra light, especially if the tracing is bold and clear. Be sure that any color added is waterproof, and be careful not to apply it too thickly or the color will plug the holes and make stitching difficult. A quick spray of clear fixative is additional insurance against the colors running onto the wool. Needlepoint should never be completely soaked when blocking or cleaning, even though waterproof supplies have been used. Scotchguard can pose other problems, which are covered in the chapter on mounting and finishing.

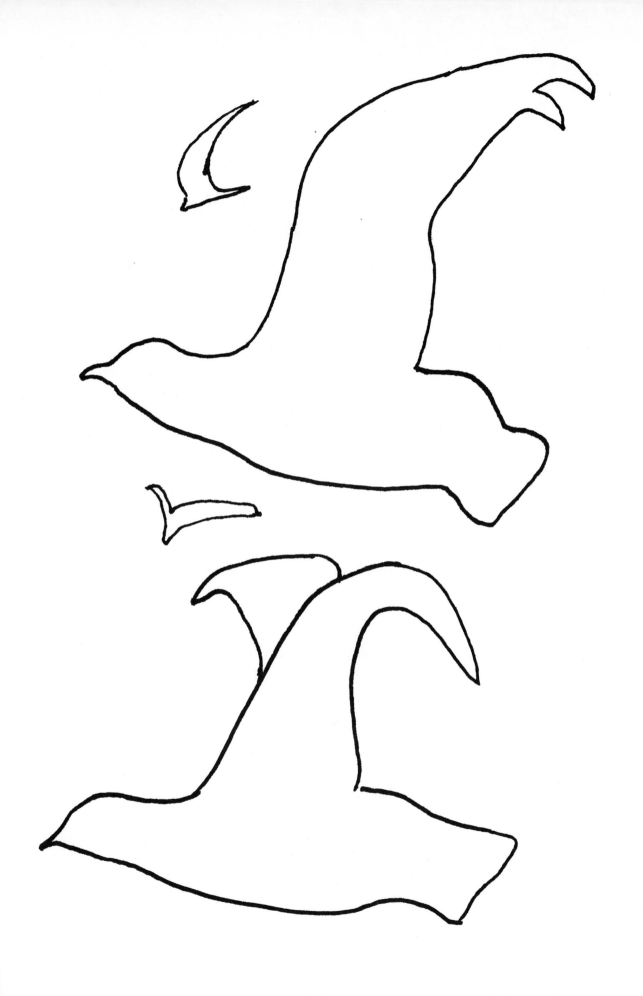

Mounting and finishing

If cleaning is necessary, have it done professionally before you block your needlepoint. Be sure to instruct the cleaner *not* to press or iron, which flattens the stitches; much texture will be lost, and nothing will be gained.

Generally, your free-form bargello piece will not require extensive blocking since it doesn't seem to lose its shape the way needlepoint done with other stitches may. There is also less chance that colors will run, since it has been worked on a blank rather than a painted canvas. You still should not soak or bathe the piece, but merely sponge it to soften the canvas sizing. Make a solution by soaking half a cake of Fels Naphtha soap in half a bucket of water for a half hour. The solution should be slippery but not thick, and the soap *must* be a naphtha soap. Never use spray starch—it draws insects and moths while the naphtha repels them.

Make your own blocking board out of ½-inch insulation board, larger than the piece to be blocked. Cover it with a layer of drill cloth or heavy muslin or canvas. This can be pulled around to the back of the board and stapled securely. A more pleasing effect can be achieved if the board is covered with checked gingham, preferably with ½-inch to 1-inch squares. If this is carefully mounted on the Upson board, the pattern forms a grid, making it unnecessary to draw vertical and horizontal lines with an indelible marker. You may find it easier to glue the material lightly on the Upson board before stapling it on the back; any white glue or wallpaper glue will serve. Gingham gives the board a gayer appearance, both in use and in storage. If the grid is being drawn on, a light spray of clear fixative will ensure its permanence.

Place the needlepoint right side down on an ironing board or pressing board. Soak a clean cloth or part of an old sheet in the soapy solution, wring it out, and place it over the needlepoint. Steam the needlepoint lightly with an iron set accurately at "wool." This will make the needlepoint flexible so it can be returned to a perfect rectangle or square. Place the needlepoint, again face down, on the board. Using a staple gun, line up the four corners and staple them first. The piece will still appear to be puckered. Put one staple in the measured center of each side, then one in the middle of each space, until the piece is fastened very securely to the board with staples placed about 2 inches apart all the way around. This should make it lie flat. Press it again with the soap solution cloth that has been wrung out as before—never use it dripping wet—and let it stand overnight.

To remove the piece from the board, simply pull it off, without bothering to remove the staples until it is off the board. It will come off very easily.

Metallic or synthetic threads will not tolerate steam or high temperature; ideally they should be worked on a frame so that blocking is unnecessary. (See page 19 on the use of frames.) Care must also be taken with silk threads; moisture will not injure silk but heat will cause it to rot. Uneven moisture may cause water stains—desirable in watered silk fabrics, but seldom in silk needlepoint. Deep colors in silk, even the very finest French *Au Vers à Soie*, are not entirely waterproof and it is best to test them for bleeding before use. Wet a strand and rub it on a white piece of cloth or paper. If color is transferred, try to find a substitute.

Scotchguard and other soil-resistant products can be used successfully if great caution is observed in the amount used. Several coats of extremely light spray are tolerable, but any heavy soaking which penetrates the wool down to the paint, no matter how waterproof, will dissolve the paint and lift it, causing it to run and blur the stitched wool—surely a disaster that can be avoided simply by following directions.

The finished, blocked needlepoint can be handled like any other piece of upholstery fabric. Do not cut the unworked areas too close to the finished areas, especially on woven canvas, which unravels with wear. A very light application of white glue around the outside edge of the finished needlepoint will also insure against unraveling. Be careful not to apply the glue so heavily that it seeps through from the back to the right side of the stitching. Rather than using a brush, dip your finger into the diluted glue and softly rub it into the wrong side of the needlepoint; this should give the necessary amount. Too much will also stiffen the work, making it harder to manage.

If the piece is to be used as a rug or wall hanging, an attractive edging can be added by wrapping heavy welting with the background color of yarn. It must be tightly bound and then stitched by hand to the turned finished edge. If the choice between rug and wall hanging has not been made, a solution that offers some versatility is to stitch a tunnel into the backing material (usually burlap, linen, or canvas). A dowel can then be placed through the tunnel and hung on café curtain hooks. It is easily removed if you choose to place the wall hanging on the floor. A light layer of latex, applied after blocking, is suggested for the back of the needlepoint if it is to be used as a rug. It increases durability and helps the piece retain the blocked shape.

Yarn color designations

	Beginning with the center color each time:
Plate 1	Paternayan 050, Colbert 61, Paternayan 242, Paternayan 843, Craft 19, Craft 20, Paternayan 853, Paternayan 050.
Plate 2	Paternayan 870, Paternayan 853, Craft 20, Craft 19, Paternayan 843, Paternayan 242, Colbert 61, Paternayan 050.
Plate 3	Paternayan 232, Paternayan 288, Paternayan 831, Paternayan G-37, Paternayan 570, Paternayan 555, Paternayan 505, Paternayan 506.
Plate 4	All Colbert: 103, 124, 123, 162, 171, 31, 169, 103.
Plate 5	All Colbert: 123, 169, 31, 171, 162, 124, 123, 103.
Plate 6	Craft 95, Paternayan B-43, Paternayan 395, Craft 118, Paternayan 385, Craft 116.
Plate 7	Colbert 117, Colbert 113, Colbert 116, Colbert 131, Colbert 129, Craft 74, Craft 95.

The following pages of graph paper can be used to help you chart your own designs. May I suggest that you cut one out and have copies made. I find it very handy to have a pad of them ready whenever inspiration strikes.

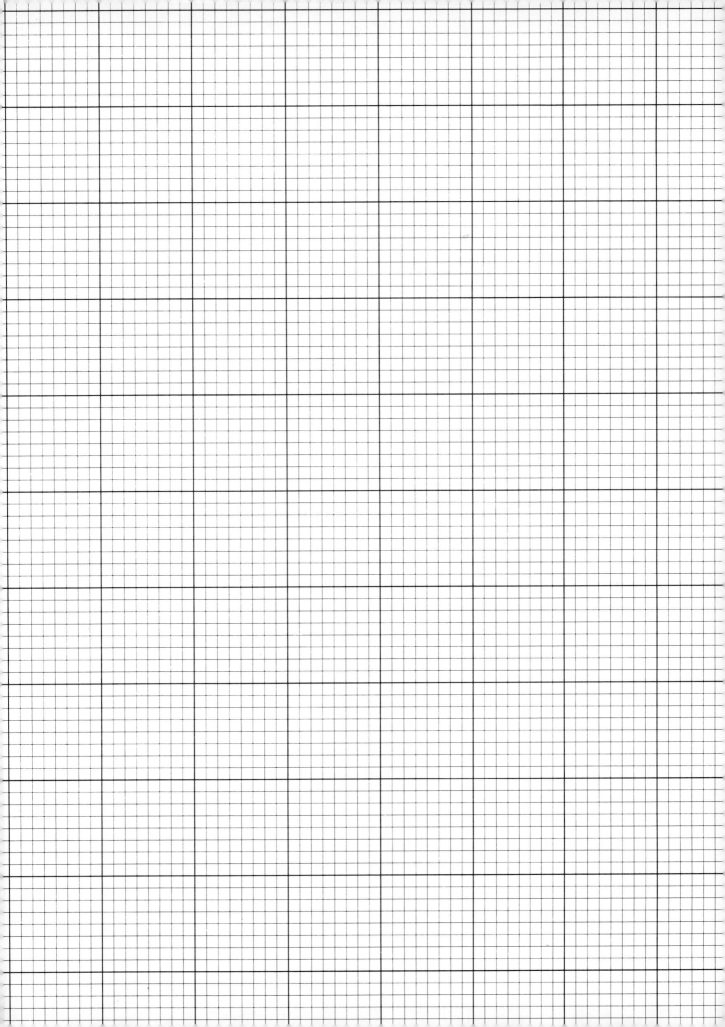

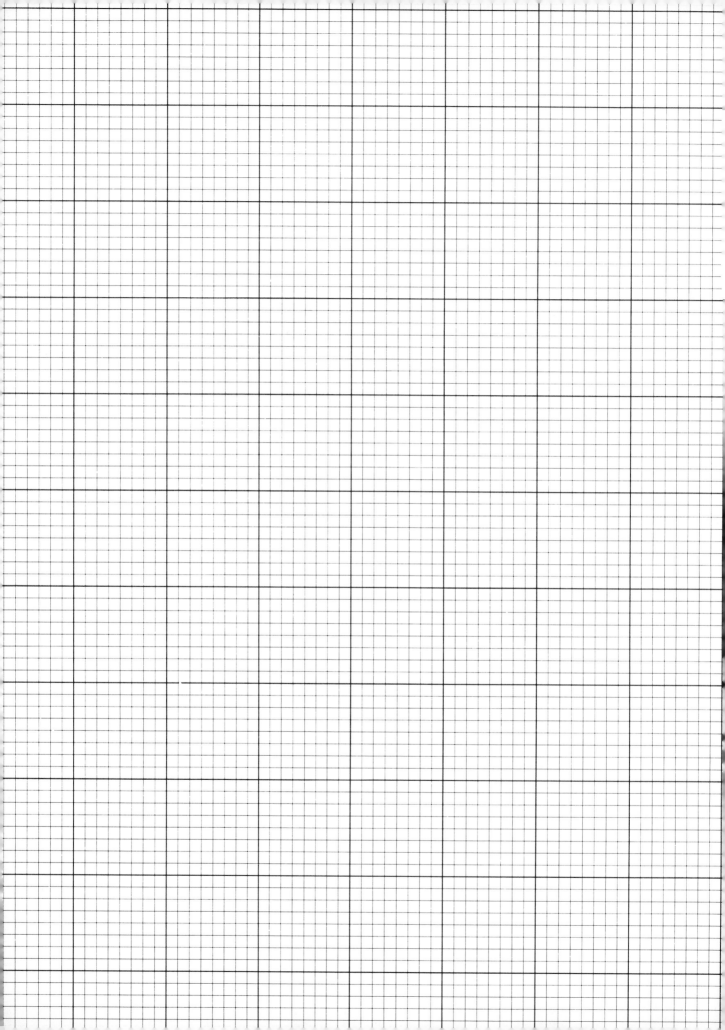

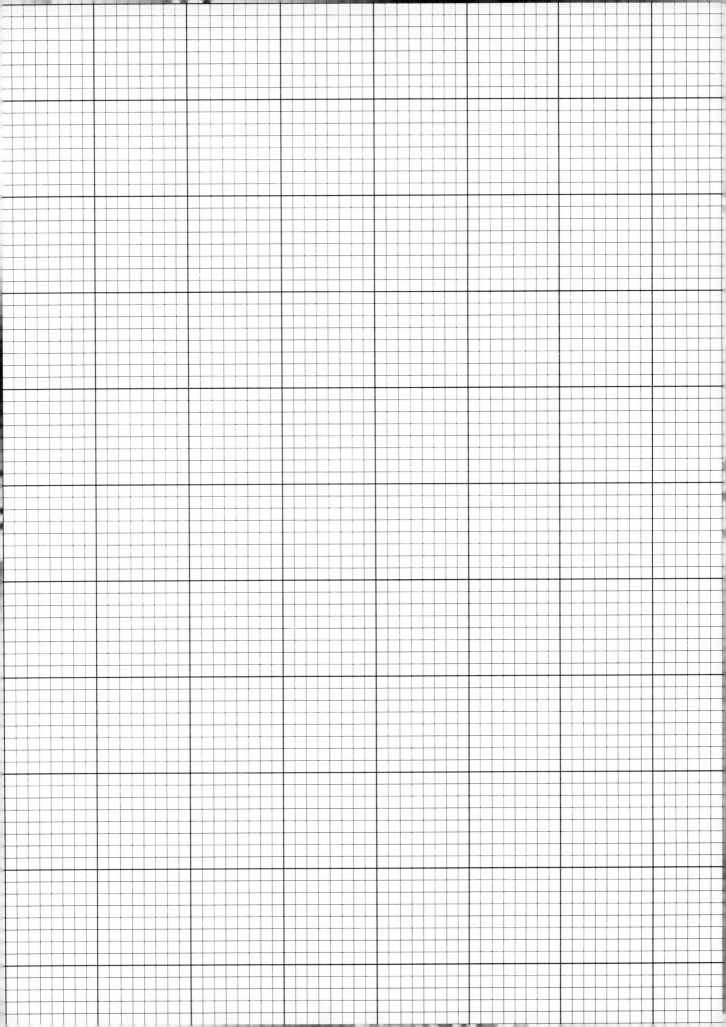

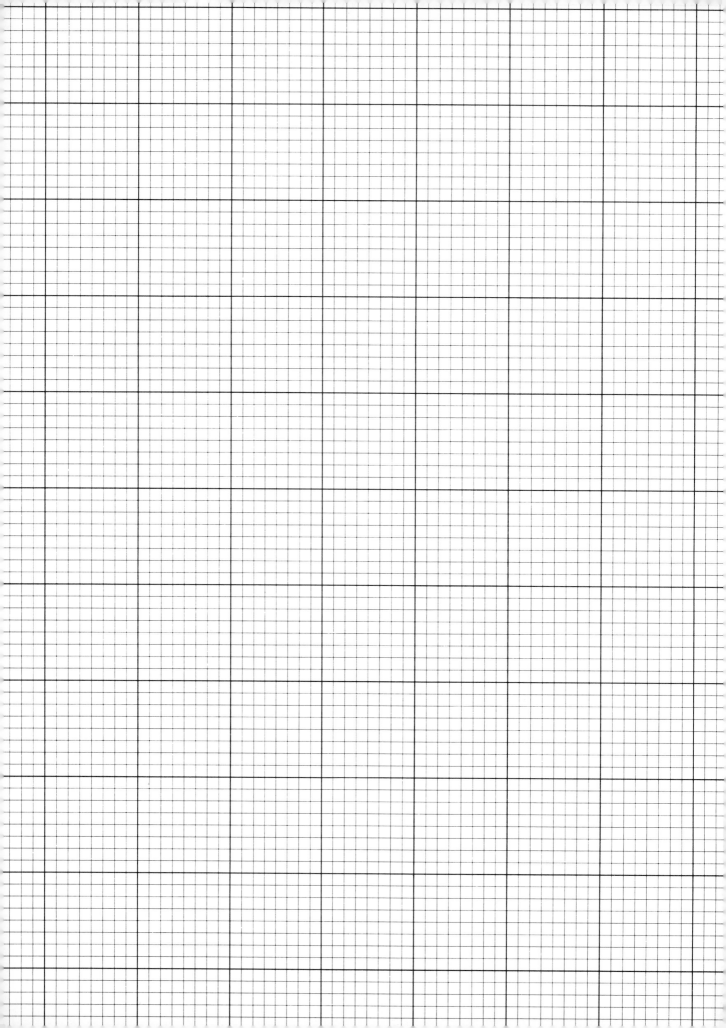

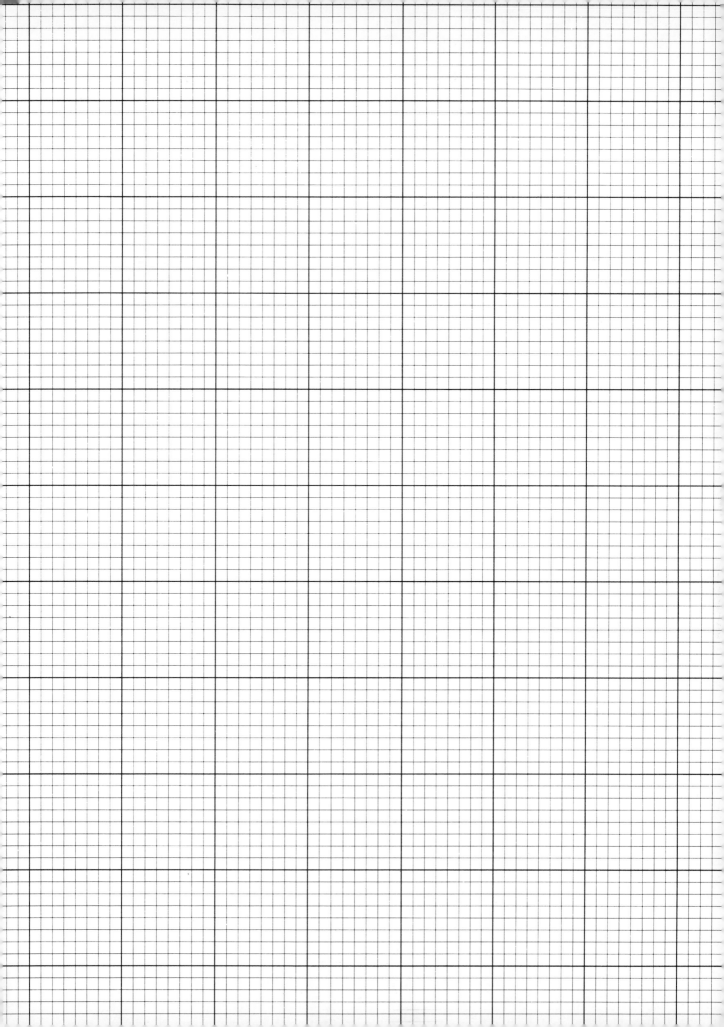

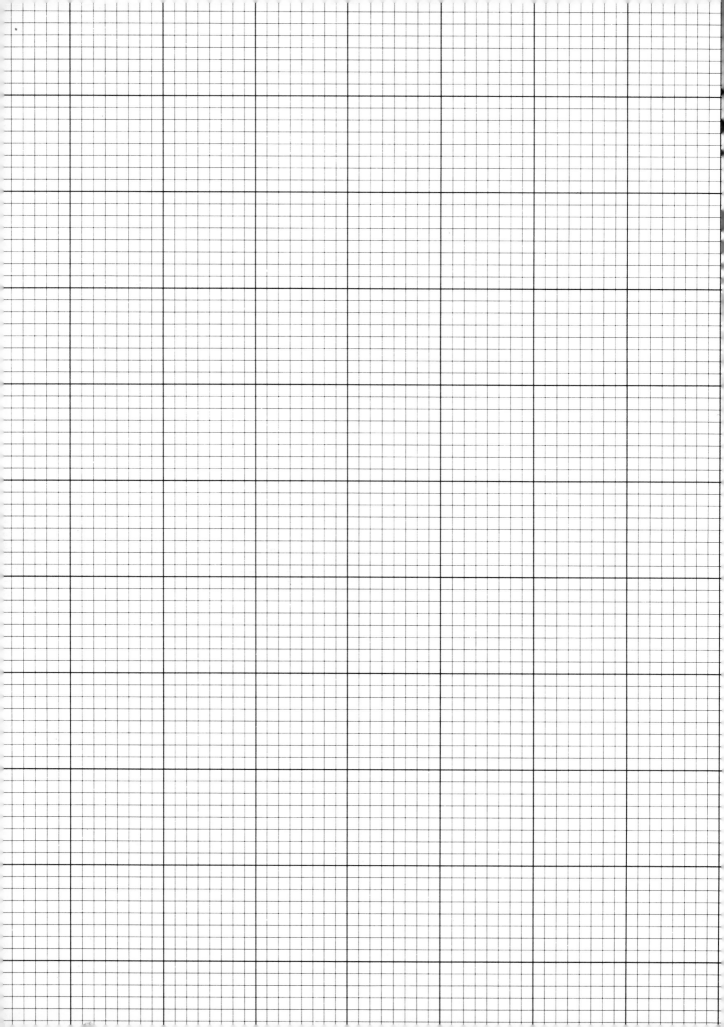